17

To Linda, David, & Family,

The Author of this Book is A
Friend of mine, & its her First. Everyone
I have given it to over the last
few months is loving it, & my
hope is that you will as well.
You are a terrific Family
that Contributes much to PCNP.

Hope your trip to Mexico was
fulfilling & fun, & that your
Foot heals quickly.
Enjoy, & God Bless each
& all.   Love,
— Barbara Reebe —

30 VISITS WITH GOD

Drawing closer for breakthrough

SIMPLE • LOVING • LIFE CHANGING

by

Jeannie Settembre

bush PUBLISHING & associates

ISBN: 978-1-944566-09-8

Bush Publishing & Associates books may be ordered at www.BushPublishing.com or www.Amazon.com. For further information, please contact:
Bush Publishing & Associates
www.BushPublishing.com

Editor: Blue Square and JoeLynn Daugherty

Art Direction and Graphic Design: Mary-Ann Ellsworth / Truth Boost

Because of the dynamic nature of the Internet, any web address or link contained in this book may have changed since publication and may no longer be valid.

This book is dedicated to Fiore...

*My best friend, husband and partner
in life and ministry*

TABLE OF CONTENTS

INTRODUCTION

Time Well Spent for Breakthrough

It's **certainly no coincidence** or happenstance that you have chosen to read *30 Visits with God*. Why? Because God will always place new and simple ways, especially for you, to draw you closer to His perfect plan for your life.

Only God, through His Word, can bring about what's best for you and *30 Visits with God* is nothing more than a contemporary look into the Book of Psalms and the loving journey we can all relate to as we come closer to the One who loves us the most.

So whether you choose a morning visit to anchor your soul so it doesn't drift too far away during the day or you need something to spark a conversation as you draw the curtains on the world at night, this book and the challenge it represents, will surely foster a new and stirring intimacy for you.

I have been tremendously impacted by the time I've chosen to dedicate to the Lord, and as I wrote *30 Visits with God*, my daily prayer was that you would experience how simple and joyful it is to give Him just a little extra attention each day. Keep in mind as you read, that a purposeful visit with Him won't take you any longer than it takes to watch your favorite television program or even prepare dinner. It's time well spent before the Lord.

I want you to feel good about yourself and your decision, because choosing 30 visits with Him, proves that you have chosen just one more simple way among many that says, "yes" to His wonderful plan for your life.

I'll be praying for you!

—Jeannie Settembre

CHAPTER 1

In a very short while, I'm going to pass the baton so the Holy Spirit can take over and start you on a journey you've probably never thought possible. It's your time to step over the threshold and into the chamber of the Lord, where amazing things will begin to happen in your world. God has your answers and He's waiting to take you by the hand, sit you down and reveal all you need to know about Him, yourself and others. He's heard you knocking, sees the whole picture and knows just what to do to get you to the places you want to go. Give Him 30 days to prove it.

30 Visits with God is written in the form of a letter to you each day where God will speak to your deepest concerns, say something that will heal your hurts, and also give you direction to achieve what you thought was impossible. Then it's your turn to respond to Him. There are thought provoking questions included for you. They will make you think and give you an opportunity to talk to God.

30 Visits with God is a special place where you and your God can meet and work it all out. You will be blessed because you came. So now, child of the Most High…here is your Lord. Go ahead, take His hand, go with Him to your secret place…you'll never be the same.

CHAPTER 2

Thirty days is all I (God) need to cause some serious changes in your life. If you're wondering why things are sometimes so difficult to handle and you know there's got to be more, you're on the right track already! There surely is something more waiting for you, and you've come to the right place to find out exactly what it is.

Let's take the next step. Let's spend some quality time together over the next 30 days. If we do, you'll come to conclusions about some of life's toughest issues and our time together will be worth every minute you spend with Me.

I took My disciples and others out of the crowd and had intimate times of conversation with them. It was in those conversations with Me that everything began to make sense in their lives. Our daily chats caused great growth within them and gave way to greater intimacy and direction. I want to do the same for you. You are My modern-day disciple and I want you to emerge from our conversations deeply rooted in truths that can and will set you free.

The next 30 days will be filled with insights necessary for your life to become fruitful and prosperous in every way. You asked Me for something you could do to draw closer to Me—and here it is!

The psalmists have walked this road with Me into a deeper and more intimate relationship and it's your turn now. They were never the same and you won't be either. Whether you've been a faithful follower for quite some time or if I'm just beginning to pique your interest, you're going to come up a level in your understanding of Me.

It's My Spirit that caused you to pick up this invitation and it's My same Spirit that will accompany you as you turn the pages. So many people have created their own version of who I am. Let's clear the smoke and bring clarity once and for all. Like any good conversation, I'll speak and then help you express your feelings too. That's what conversation is all about, isn't it... an intimate time of getting together and sharing.

You'll never be the same. How could you be? I, your Heavenly Father, have called you. I, Jesus, have made the way possible; and I, your Holy Spirit, am here to guide you every step of the way!

I want to show you how relevant the Book of Psalms is and how it still has a thing or two to say about your life. As we look at the raw emotions of the psalmists together, you will see how candidly they brought Me their trials, sorrows and excitements in life. We can use them as a springboard for you to tell Me all about what's going on in your life and we will figure it out together. I've been waiting for this day.

You were created to spend time with Me. Are you humble enough to give it a try? Then let's go because an understanding of Me and My Word brings Light, and He who searches finds.

Happy searching! Happy finding!

ONE

The Start of Something Big

– Psalm 1 –

The **Psalms of David** are a vast storehouse of many experiences and emotions that played out during the course of David's turbulent lifetime. With each turn of events, David found solace and strength in documenting his emotions, which accompanied both mountaintop adventures and the pain he experienced in the depths of life's emotional valley. Psalm 1 gives you an insight into some of the truths he painfully and joyously acquired along the way. They're truths that, if taken with a measure of humility, will help you steer clear of some common land mines of life, and also give you a good indication of how to effectively venture through anything that comes your way.

Learn from David. He's a master of the school of life's highs and lows and how to believe in Me and trust in the promise of victory that was won on the cross for each and every circumstance of his life.

He says in Psalm 1:1-2, "Blessed is the man who does not walk in the counsel of the wicked or stand in the way of sinners or sits in the seat of mockers. But his delight is in the law of the Lord and on this law he meditates day and night.

For the Lord watches over the way of the righteous, but the way of the wicked will perish."

Can you see how David begins this Psalm with expressions of joy? That's because there's joy in obeying Me and freedom in refusing to listen to those who ridicule both you and Me. You can surely rest knowing that by following Me you will have the freedom to become the person I create you to be.

In Psalm 1, I contrast the saint from the sinner and the wicked from the righteous. I make the distinction between those who strive to stay close to me and those who consider Me a restraint upon their lives.

If you notice, it's all spelled out for you here and how obedience and the discipline of reading My Word is in strong contrast to the nonchalant attitude of so many. Don't be afraid of the word "discipline" it only means that you seek to "throw off everything that hinders you" and come into my presence with an expectancy for greatness and peace beyond your wildest dreams.

Disciplined times of reading is the way I've chosen to reveal Myself. There's no substitute for it. It's the only way for you to truly know Me. People often think they're free because they keep their distance from Me. They think they've broken free from chains and bondage, but little do they know that they are still serving something. It could be money or perhaps their position in life. It could be anything at all. My child, the only way to true freedom is paved with My Word. To look anywhere else is a waste of time.

As you sit with Me and spend some time, I'll do My part and reveal all you need to know to live the abundant life I died to give you.

If you want to truly withstand all the evil of this life here on earth, let Me make it easy for you. You have only one thing to accomplish in your day. Here are your marching orders: Read My Word, think about what you have read. Then sit for a while and allow it to sink into your being. That's it! Don't worry about anything else. Leave the rest to Me. It's up to Me to remind you to read and to teach you how to apply my truths to your life. You do your part and I'll do mine. If you expect Me to, I'll send my Holy Spirit to make what you read come alive for you.

If you decide to take Me up on my offer, you won't find yourself falling prey and easily persuaded by the mockers, scorners and the foolishness of life that David speaks of. In My Word lies the secret of a strong and satisfying life that's really worth living. My Words have the power to ground you. They'll build you up and fortify your dreams.

You'll acquire answers to your biggest questions and know where to find my truth. Everything is there within the pages of my Word. There are things I have to tell you that won't come through any other means but your reading and thinking about My Word. Don't you want to hear the special and personal things I have to say to you? If you do, then come as you are!

I want to give you life-changing insights that will surely set you on the right path. Will you trust Me? Then come. Let's begin to do what you were created for...to have an intimate relationship with Me your God and Savior.

Give Me your thoughts now on something important. What things in life are most important to you? Stop and think about it for a minute or two. Don't rush!

Pause and tell Me.

Now, what are some of your desires in life? The ones that are based in love and desire change for the good. Take your time and think about it.

What you're thinking right now is very important to Me. You see, I planted those desires for peace and joy, abundance and favor in you Myself before you were born, and I long to make them happen. We can make them happen. Together we can dilute your fleshly desires to nothing so great things can really start to emerge. And the great thing is these wonderful desires based in love are not only for you, but will spill out of your life and on to others.

Now what about sadness...talk to Me about what makes you feel down. Again, take your time. I want to heal you. Don't be afraid.

Do you think spending a little more time together with Me each day will benefit you? Why not spend the rest of your day as you go about your routine thinking about our time together and how it's the first of many that will bring you joy and victory.

I'm glad you came today and remember wherever you go, I go also! I'm right there with you every minute of your day.

TWO

The Power of Asking

— Psalm 2 —

In **Psalm 2 we** find David sharing what I said to him during a time of great questioning in his life. As he looked around, many nations were gathering with one thing in common: rebellion against Me. This disturbed him greatly; and as you look around your world today you, too, are witnessing a great and mighty force of rebellion throughout the nations. You can read in Psalm 2 both David's question and My answer to the dilemma that plagued his time and continues to plague yours. I've documented the solution. It's simple: just "Ask of Me."

Psalm 2:8 says to "Ask of Me and I will give you the heathen for thine inheritance and the utter most parts of the earth for your possession."

Listen to what I am offering you here. All you need to do is "Ask of Me."

For you who can find it within your heart to look outside yourself and cry out on behalf of other suffering nations, I give you My Word that, if you ask, you will receive My "yes and amen" on their behalf.

Just think about it! Because My Holy Spirit is prompting you to pray for the lost and suffering, and you take Me up on My offer, nations will receive the glorious benefits. Peace will be instilled in their borders, children will be nourished, hearts will turn toward Me and Salvations will be won! All the things that I am blamed for in this world will be taken care of. They didn't happen because of Me and together, just because you and people like you come and ask, I will change and heal you and your land.

Food and medical supplies will penetrate the iron walls that are formed around My people, preventing them from receiving their basic needs. The evil that has My precious children within its grip will be pried open by your intercession on their behalf.

I have a plan for all nations, from the desolate to the wealthy. I have the solution to the poverty and greed that keeps them in bondage and devoid of my blessings. I respond to prayer and I'm moved by your persistence in order to set them free.

Your prayers don't have to be long and lengthy. They just need to be heartfelt. I'll use them to equip missionaries with the perseverance they need to reach all nations. I'll even plant inside the hearts of future missionaries the desire to come and set the captives free. Your prayers cause their hearts to hear Me and respond. You and I can call them to the mission field and equip them with everything they need. All their needs are met because you've asked.

"Ask Me today and I will give you the nations as an inheritance and the uttermost parts as your possessions."

Take Me up on My offer, so the nations' hunger for Me, both physical and spiritual, will be satisfied! The atrocities that prevail throughout their land will come under My subjection and their victory is assured. All because you took the time to intercede for them and trusted Me enough to deny yourself for a moment.

There isn't a nation on the planet that's beyond my power to heal and save. Pick one and pray. Cry out today for your friends, allies and enemies. Don't miss the opportunity I've placed before you. Great things are accomplished and change will occur because you "Ask of Me."

Here's something for you to think about for the rest of the day:

I have a special place in My heart for those who trust Me with their own needs and take the time to lift up others. How greatly your faith is expressed when you turn from your own cares and seek My face, even for those you don't know. Take a step of faith today. Turn away from the things that trouble you the most and trust Me. And while you're praying for the nations, I promise I will surely rain down My provisions for you. Your breakthrough will be part of the inheritance.

Think big on their behalf and My River of love will flow into impoverished areas and places that cannot be penetrated any other way. I know what you need. I have you, your family, even your nation, under My careful watch. I promise in My Word that you will do greater things than I did while on earth. This is it!

Ask and I will give you the nations. One day you'll meet them in heaven and they'll thank you for bringing salvation to their land! So take the focus off yourself and lift up a foreign nation today. It will feel great and accomplish much!

Open your eyes to what I'm offering. It's an offer of life change for you and for them. I've endued you with power to do great things. Let's change the world together and take possession of a land that desperately needs your prayers.

What personal concerns occupy your thoughts and prayer times the most? Selah...that means stop and think about it for a while. Can you trust Me that I've heard all your prayers and will not disappoint you?

Can you pray for another nation today with the fervency that you pray for your own troubles? What nation will it be? They're waiting for the freedom you and I can bring to their land. Tomorrow will be a glorious day with Me for you personally, but just for today, let's heal a desolate land.

THREE

You Are Safe

– Psalm 3 –

Psalm 3 describes gut-wrenching times for King David, but at least he knew where to bring his sorrow and pain. David was literally escaping death at every turn. His throne had been seized and there was a plan set for his execution. As he fled from the land he once ruled as king, he cried out to Me in desperation. He called, I answered and I became the Shield about him in his time of need. I made sure that not a hair on his head was touched by his enemies.

Psalm 3:3-4 is David declaring, "But You are a Shield around me, O Lord, You are my Glory and the Lifter of my head. To the Lord I cried aloud and He answered Me from His Holy Hill."

Here's the story. David was running for his life. He was now a fugitive king. His very own son, Absalom, that he loved dearly had just claimed his kingdom, forced him out and would not be satisfied until David was dead. He had an army hunting for him like a wild animal. And it was his army. They were a fickle and blood-thirsty crowd for sure, and they had now set their sights on David and his small band of devoted soldiers. Isn't it the most hurtful kind of pain when those you love or those who are supposed to love you mount up against you?

These were desperate times for David. Painful times, times of rejection and times of fear. One wrong move and his life would be over.

Well, David had a member of his small army that made all the difference in the world: Me. I was with him every step of the way. I was his Shield. I gave him ultimate protection because he humbled himself and asked Me to lead the way. I knew just what he should do, what course of action he should take, when to move and when to be still.

I watched over him closely and revealed the plots of his enemy. I empowered him with strategies that were fail-proof. I was all he needed. You see, I sit on My Holy Hill and I'm aware of all things. My children have nothing to fear. Did you hear Me? You have nothing to fear.

Do you know that I always have you under my watchful eye? I'm aware of everything that has anything to do with you. I'm aware of the smallest details of your life, and I have an insight into your troubles like no other.

Sometimes things can get so bad and spin out of control so much that all you can do is lift your head and cry out to Me. When all your strength is gone, and even if you're desperate, there's hope. You really have no idea how much I love you. You might have some indication, but even if you've spent a lifetime reading My Word, your knowledge hasn't exhausted my deep and abiding love for you; and I still have so much more to tell you. I'm not intimidated, affected or impressed by the number of issues in your life, nor the power of your enemies. I am the solution to it all.

I AM your great and mighty Shield. I AM all around you. You're right in the middle of my surrounding wall of protection. It's like a moat of fire. Nothing will dare scale My wall of protection. It's powerful and protects you in ways that are beyond your understanding right now, but as you continue to sit with Me you'll come to know it quite well. I've spared your life several times. You're alive for a reason and you're perfectly and completely safe with Me.

David said to Me, "Many are saying of me, 'God will never deliver him.'" Let me tell you something; you don't have to listen to the naysayers whose words and advice to you are prompted by their negative hearts. They may try and persuade you into believing that I don't want to or that I'm incapable of bringing victory into your life. I AM capable and I AM willing to see you through. I AM your Shield and I long to be the Lifter of your head. Look to me and there will be no reason for you to hang your head in despair.

Don't you remember when you cried out to me in times of trouble in the past?

Let me remind you of My love for you and how I've seen you through many times over. Let me have the opportunity to remind you each day how much I long to be your Guide and Shield throughout your lifetime. When you are down, feeling alone, and saddened or defeated, I'll lift your head and I'll lift it high!

Come to Me and lay your needs and fears before me. I am waiting to flood your situation with My solution. Cast them upon Me and leave My chamber with peace. You don't have to carry it any longer. Selah. Stop and think about what I've just said to you.

You won't be able to explain what's happening, but you will be able spend your day in peace and then go to bed and sleep a beautiful and restful sleep each night. Your enemy may have lots of power and influence, but you have

Me, your One true God. I died on the cross to earn the right to be your Shield. My Name is Jesus and I am all of these things and more!

You have called out to Me as David did, and I hear you and I am answering you. I'll destroy anything that is not of Me in your life. I'm the only One from whom deliverance flows. I and I alone will surely see you through.

Come here. Come closer to Me and ask yourself, has anyone disappointed you similar to the way David's son Absalom disappointed him? Take some time and allow Me to scan your life with you.

I didn't create you to carry the burden of disappointment and rejection. It's too heavy and too much. I want to be your solution and healing. It is only because of My great love that you're not totally consumed by the disappointments that this life can bring. My love for you is new every morning and My faithfulness towards you is beyond your wildest dreams.

Let Me in. Let Me help. Now is the time for Me to wash all the rejection and disappointment away! Stay awhile! Just sit and let Me love you.

I'm glad you came and spent some time with Me. We can accomplish a lot as we sit together day by day. There's a whole new world waiting for you! Take up your Shield! Place Me between you and fear, between you and disease, between you and anything that comes your way.

FOUR

A Beautiful and Restful Night's Sleep

– Psalm 4 –

David was still on the run. Danger was lurking everywhere. The glory of his kingship had been reduced to
nothing but shame, and the thought of his son and faithful followers turning against him was simply too much for
him to handle. He was drained physically, emotionally and
spiritually. Then he called on Me, and before he finished
speaking he was able to lie down for a peaceful rest.

Psalm 4:1- "Answer me when I call you, O my God. Give
me relief from my distress; be merciful to me and hear my
prayer." Psalm 4:8- "I will lie down and sleep in peace, for
you alone, O Lord, make me dwell in safety."

How do you think David, in the midst of all this turmoil,
could lay down calmly and sleep? Most people would be
up all night tossing and turning on their beds. The answer
is simple. David's faith and confidence wasn't in himself or
even in his band of soldiers. He wasn't even pipe-dream-
ing that perhaps Absalom would change his mind and call
off his manhunt. None of this could assure a good night's
sleep. His confidence was in Me. He had learned early on
that I would indeed answer him when he called.

David's satisfaction came in knowing that it was Me who watches over him. Seeking anything else would be a pure waste of time. He had Me, and no back up was necessary. This kind of peace and assurance is your portion too, so go to bed tonight and as you put your head on the pillow, I'll remind you of the peace and love that awaits you each night. Let Me convince you that true relief and protection are surely possible. Your situations are safe with Me.

The relief I want to give you has the power to permeate every facet of your life. All anxiety, fear and disillusions that trouble you will be overtaken and bound if you allow Me to touch your life the way I desire to.

My peace isn't some temporary truce that will satisfy for a brief period of time. That's what the world offers you - a temporary pause for your mind and body. You know there's no real and lasting relief in that. And you also know, deep in your heart, that there's something so much better than what you feel right now. You know it because you have been created for it. Come and taste the better portion. My peace for you stems from My desire to calm every storm and ease your troubled heart. Let's make an indescribable peace within your heart our goal.

Everything was silenced when I rebuked the storm for my disciples. My order for it to fall under My obedience was swift and powerful. Everything was shut down as it came under my subjection. I said, "Peace. Be still!" Everything raging against My disciples collapsed under my command. I can do the same for you.

My peace carries with it a settling of your soul and a calming of your spirit, so you can fall into my arms and sleep a perfect and restful sleep. You surely can lie down and sleep in peace as David testified, and from that sleep you will awake and remain in My loving hand all day long.

You see, My dear precious one, it's your spirit that needs to be calmed first and then the relaxing of your body and your mind will follow. Let's put first things first. Let me calm your spirit as only I can. You've struggled to find something that will free you from fear and anxiety and have even found some temporary relief at times, but you've been going about it in the wrong way. Your attempts to obtain peace are skewed. Don't seek ways to calm your body and mind when the most important thing is to calm your spirit. That's how addictions are formed.

You were created to go through this life in perfect peace, no matter what's going on around you. "Seek Me first and all things, including perfect peace, will be added unto you." Sit with Me and read My Word and I will fill your spirit to overflowing. I will answer you when you call and give you relief from your distress. I long to be merciful to you and I really do hear you when you pray.

As you call on Me and rest in my embrace, you'll be able to release your worries, fears and concerns and they will obey my order to be silenced forever. You can be sure that I want to fill you with my solution for everything that concerns you. Come collapse in my arms. Don't be afraid. You were created to dwell here.

I have heard you even when you didn't know you were calling. Tears are liquid prayers, you know. And guess what, I've even heard you when you were walking away from me.

All of your wandering was just a desperate search for Me. You've found Me now. I'm glad. My arms are open. I've waited so long for you to come and I'm elated that you're finally here. Rest for a while within my embrace. I said rest. It's where you belong and what you've been missing.

This is our special place. What's troubling you today? Talk to Me. When you simply tell Me what's going on in your own words, I receive it as the highest form of prayer.

What is it? I'm here to listen and I'm here to cause change. I can and I will. Try just sitting quietly in My arms. It's a safe place. It's the secret place you've heard about.

FIVE

A Fresh Start Is Waiting

– Psalm 5 –

While still **suffering the** pressure and reality of losing everything, David resorted to the One Stability in his life, and that's Me. He was rejected by so many. Absalom was in full motion and successfully influencing his army that the death of David was their goal. He and his army vowed to continue their pursuit and wouldn't stop until David was dead. But take a look at what David said to Me.

Remember how he bedded himself down in Psalm 4 the night before and slept like a child without a care in the world? Well now, here he is awakening, refreshed and fully confident that I would see him through yet another day.

David praises Me in Psalm 5:3 and says, "In the morning, O Lord, you hear my voice; in the morning I lay my requests before you and wait in expectation." And in Psalm 5:12 he says, "For surely, O Lord, You bless the righteous. You surround them with Your favor as with a shield."

Come and follow the example of My friend David and seek me in the morning hours because it's a special window of time that's saturated with my grace and mercies for you. I watch over you with My watchful eye all night long and I wait for you to awaken each morning.

As you open your eyes and we start our day together, I want you to realize that a new opportunity is upon you. I'm right here to greet you and cover you afresh with My love and all that it entails. A great gift is waiting. Whatever you need is here. When I say "whatever you need," I'm talking about the salvation of everything that has to do with you.

You see, salvation has many facets. It's not just a reservation for heaven, it's really a treasure box filled with all sorts of expressions of My love. They're all the things you want and need right now. Open it up. There's peace for you in my salvation. There's freedom from the things that bind and restrict you and there's provision beyond your comprehension. So wipe the sleep from your eyes, untie the bow, lift the lid and take what you need. I've secured it all for you and present it to you each morning. Go ahead! Open it right now. My salvation treasure box is filled with all you need for your day.

Arise and call me your King and your God each morning as David did, because you surely have My attention in that special time of your awakening. Do you want to live and move and have your being infilled with My provisions each day? Then reach for Me while your day is young.

Don't even put your foot on the floor for even that is an effort made by you that needs the prelude of my love and direction. I want you to be aware of this special time of intimacy with Me because David was right. "All those who take refuge in Me will be glad." (verse 11) You can sing for joy because you love My Name and take refuge in Me each morning.

What is my name? What will you call me today? Do you need Me to provide for you? Then call Me your Provider. Call Me your Comforter, so I can wipe out your fear and pain. Or how about your Prince of Peace? What do you need? Whatever it is, that's my Name.

Read a small portion of truth that's found in My Word. I'll direct you to the promises I want you to know. I will clothe you with protection and favor so you can go forth fully assured that I've secured your day in My will.

Receive My Glory Light. It's the same light that lit up the face of Moses. You'll be radiant as you go about your day no matter what trials you're facing. My Glory Light blinds the enemy of your soul and shows you the way.

Your fears and doubt are unnecessary and futile. I'll see you through with my direction and peace. Start your day knowing you've reached for Me and now there will be special times throughout your day. I'll interrupt those doubts and fears with the very portion of Scripture I have directed you to. Expect it. Because I want the very best for you.

Let me ask you. How do you wake-up in the morning? Is there something painful and worrisome that's starts to erode your peace as soon as you open your eyes? As it begins to arise in your mind, let it rise up and leave your spirit. I'm calling it out. Take My love instead.

There's not a moment in time that I am not with you, aware of your troubles and pouring out My love upon you. You have the freedom to tell me anything. Let your first moments of consciousness be a connecting of our spirits. Together we can take on anything the world serves up. Wherever you go today, I'm with you. Why not just sit a little while longer with Me now and receive. I've set a beautiful banquet before you. Take. Eat.

SIX

Finally... Some Relief

– Psalm 6 –

David was still facing a lot of heartache and his emotions were fluctuating rapidly in Psalm 6. One minute he felt as if he was being plunged into the depths of darkness and despair without a shred of hope and then, even though his troubles hadn't changed, things seem to lighten up a bit.

When David wrote this Psalm, he was crying out to Me in one of the most painful times of his life. I met him in that anguish. There's no depth of pain that could exceed my reach and in his darkest hour, I was there.

He cries in Psalm 6:2, "Be merciful to Me, Lord, for I am faint; Oh Lord, heal me for my bones are in agony. Psalm 6:4 says, "Turn O Lord, and deliver me; save me because of Your unfailing love."

This was David's cry when he found himself filled with sickness, anguish and torment. His cry was a piercing wail of hopelessness and desperation. He had come to the end of himself and was crying out for a release from unbearable agony. His torment was two-fold. He had contracted a serious illness (His bones were in agony) and if that weren't enough, My prophet Nathan had just visited him and exposed his sinfulness concerning his affair with Bathsheba and the death of her innocent husband Uriah.

Nathan's reminder came as a shock. He thought he had put all of that behind him. He thought he'd figured things out, smoothed things over and moved on. Now, here comes one of My prophets to shake things up and stir it all up again. I had to send Nathan because he didn't listen to the conviction of My Holy Spirit. Sure, he seemed to be moving on, but I loved him too much to allow unrepentant sin to continue to cause sickness in His body.

David didn't say a word in his defense when he was confronted by Nathan. He couldn't. You can learn from David. He stood convicted. Nathan's rebuke penetrated his prideful heart, pierced his soul and brought him to his knees.

You see, Nathan was just completing a work that had already been started. Deep within David, things hadn't been resolved at all, and it was wreaking havoc with his body and his emotions. Something was unsettled, and on another level he knew it. But he responded to my call and fell to his knees in sincerity, and the depth of his sorrow released him from the agony within his bones.

Let Me take you through a process today.

David called Me into his sin, guilt and torment, and I did indeed forgive and heal him with my unfailing love. And I will surely do the same for you. That sickness in your body, and that unsettled feeling, it can only be cured by resolving things with Me. I didn't bring it upon you. It's a matter of some unresolved sin or deep hurt within your heart that has nowhere else to go. It makes its home within your body and disquiets your emotions.

Bring Me your hurts and sinfulness with humility, and I'll rescue you also from all guilt and the things that torment you. Something great will transpire within your soul when you do. My forgiveness will flush out years of agony. My forgiveness will heal your illness.

I'm telling you this today because I want you to have the same gift I gave David. Bow down. Admit to Me humbly that you've sinned. Ask Me about your wounded soul. Talk to Me and I'll reveal the real source of your pain. Let Me in now so I can show you what you've missed and rain down My Spirit upon your life.

Selah. Take a minute right here. Receive relief.

Now think about this. You might be wondering why and are frustrated because you always seem to resort to the same sinful things. You plan on doing things right, but find yourself taking a step backwards. I know you're trying. I know you want to draw closer, but there's still a place in your soul that I haven't had access to. Won't you let Me go there and touch it with My warm healing Glory Light?

It's all about forgiving yourself and others now. When I tell you that your sins are cast into the sea of forgetfulness, I mean it. You're washed as clean as a newborn baby. Won't you do the same for your offenders?

I've made it clear in My Word that your enemies are not other people. Your battles are not with flesh and blood, so let them go. Your battles have nothing to do with human beings. If they have flesh over their bones and blood coursing through their veins, they are not your enemy.

You may think that a person in your life is selfish, but they are not your enemy—selfishness is. You may be ill because someone has expressed anger or hatred towards you. It's not the person who is your enemy; it's anger and hatred! It is all coming from one source. The enemy of your soul.

A great secret to life is the knowledge that no matter what others have done to you, they're not your enemy. There's great peace in understanding what I've just said. Sure, they've allowed hurtfulness and pain to proceed from their decisions, but I will deal with that.

Stop placing your focus on other human beings. That's the problem. You're focusing on them and not Me. Let them go and live! I'll deal with them and bring them to wholeness too. Let Me create a new relationship between you and them. I can. I know what to do.

People can only hold you back if you let them. Focus on Me and let Me help.

If you obey Me and just choose to forgive those that hurt you, I'll give you the strength to tread upon the real enemies of your soul. You know the uncomfortable feeling that comes when you're around someone who's hurt you? That will diminish. You won't have any fear about being around people because all things within you have become new. They might not change, but you will. Their attacks and onslaughts may remain, but somehow you'll be unaffected by it, just as I was with the Pharisees and all who persecuted Me. Let Me make you un-offendable. Let them go.

Think about this: You've sinned greatly in your life and I've forgiven you. Did I then walk away and have nothing to do with you? Where would you be if I forgave you and then left you? I don't want you to forgive and walk away either. True forgiveness means trusting Me to take the entire brokenness of the relationship and make it unrecognizably new and different. Brand new and a blessing to all.

You can talk to Me about all those who've caused you pain, but be willing to have the relationship restored. Allow Me to make the decision of who stays in your life and who goes. You don't know if that person is an integral part of my great destiny for you. Humble yourself and find out. Can you do that?

Can you trust that I know who should be involved in your life and who shouldn't? I'll surely remove the ones who don't belong and drive them away from your midst. Cry out for mercy for your offenders. They will need it.

I see things from a different perspective than you do. Come up to My Holy Place and see things from where I sit. Don't harm My people with your unforgiveness. I haven't completed My work in them and you shouldn't be the one to hold them back.

Let's once and for all deal with your real enemies, not fallible human beings. For surely your battles aren't with flesh and blood, they're with powers and principalities and rulers of darkness and wicked things in high places!

Forgiveness is My will. I've done it for you; now do it for all who have offended you. We can't continue your growth unless you heed My word. I'll say to you what Abraham said to Pharaoh on My behalf, "Let My people go!"

If your answer is yes to My call to healing, then simply ask Me who you should forgive. You'll be surprised at the turbulence that unforgiveness is causing within you. You'll also be surprised at who I reveal. Sickness will flee from you. It's the next step for you. Come to Me willing to hear. There are people you haven't forgiven and today is your day to become free. Shhh...don't get defensive. Just let Me in.

Selah. Listen for just a while. I want to reveal who or what you should release to Me. Today is the day for you to hand your offender over to Me. I can do nothing for you until you trust Me with them. Not forgiving is basically an issue that boils down to a distrust of My justice. All those things you have been praying for are hinged on your decision to forgive.

I'm not validating what they've done. I just want you to be free. I was there when they hurt you and I cried along with you. I'm here now and asking you to let Me help you. Say yes to Me. Take a moment and release them. Your soul wounds will be healed, I promise.

SEVEN

The First Step to Freedom

– Psalm 7 –

David had many enemies. It wasn't only his son Absalom and King Saul whose hatred burned for him. Cush, the Benjamite, harbored his own hatred and plotted and schemed to cause dissension between David and King Saul. He accused David of conspiring against Saul's Kingdom and that was all that was needed to fuel an already jealous king to take action.

Cush's accusations that David sought to kill King Saul set David up for a mighty battle for his life, but David knew what to do. In this Psalm, he inquires of Me and petitions that I become the sole judge of both him and his accuser. He searched his own heart first, so he could confidently come with clean hands and a pure heart. He trusts Me enough to ask if he is somehow guilty of the charge against him. Then and only then could he ask Me to defend him and send salvation to his enemy.

That's what it really means to "take refuge in" Me and ask for deliverance.

In Psalm 7:1 David says, "O Lord My God, I take refuge in you; save and deliver me from all who pursue me." He then goes on to say in Psalm 7:17, "I will give thanks to the Lord because of his righteousness and will sing praise to the Name of the Lord Most High."

David was hard pressed on every side. His enemies were relentless and many. Their plots and schemes kept him at the foot of My throne calling out for mercy and direction both day and night. He clung to Me as if his very life depended on it, because it did.

Whenever there is success, giftedness and My anointing, there is also jealousy, accusations and attempts to send My anointed ones into a tailspin. The craftiness of the jealous is always fueled when you and others advance in My kingdom. Expect it. It's a reality of the life you are living.

Your Accuser's schemes and judgments may be violent, but so is My power and authority against every assault that comes your way. There's not an evil tongue or troublemaker that will not be exposed and disgraced on your behalf. You can be assured of that!

Before you come to Me to be your defense though, I want you to search your own heart as David did during his dilemma. He presented himself humbly before Me and asked if there was any truth to his enemies accusations? That was a great place to start. Now, he was in a position where pride had to release its grip over the situation. Humility always causes elevation and right standing with Me. Why not take a minute and bow humbly before Me?

Now let Me tell you something about getting along with others. If you ask Me to join you in all your relationships, I'll be present and by your side with even the most difficult people. It's wise to ask Me to rule and reign over all your relationships. I desire for you, Me, and the other person to be a "cord of three strands that is not easily severed." When you invite Me to be that Third Cord, I intertwine Myself into the relationship and cause it to become indestructible and a joy to behold. Go ahead, call Me into all dealings with family, friends, co-workers, even those who've treated you badly and accused you before the world.

Accusations cut like a knife, but I can be trusted. I can sort it all out.

I know whether you've been treated unfairly or if you're blinded by your self-protecting ways. Let me show you the side you don't see. Let me shine My light of understanding on you and the ones who cause you so much heartache. I know the full and intricate details and I want to reveal them to you.

I long to be the Just Judge who presides over all your interactions. I'm the only One who can sit in this seat. No one loves as I love. Therefore, no one else can stand as Mediator over the affairs of your life.

Know this truth and never forget it: Oftentimes, you're looking in the wrong direction, focusing on people and declaring them your enemy. Don't be fooled. Let me impress upon your heart once again, that if what troubles you is flesh and blood; they're not your enemy. No matter how harsh their treatment is towards you, the real enemy of your soul is hiding behind them.

You have forces against you that can only be fought in the spirit because they are spirit. Your battle is fought with forgiveness and love towards others. There's no other way, so stop trying.

David cried out for the salvation of his accusers. He asked Me to, "bring an end to violence" and to "let the assembled people gather around Me." Can you do the same? Can you cry out for the salvation and welfare of the one who has hurt you the most?

I've reserved great rewards for you if you can truly forgive and cry out for the salvation of the one who schemes and plots against you. Think about that! If you're willing, you can stand surrounded with favor and My protection, and so will they. Do you think I'll leave the relationship in the state it was when you asked? No. Everything that's not of Me will surely be demolished.

I've given you a promise in My Word that all your true spiritual enemies will be "ashamed, dismayed and turn back in sudden disgrace." You will sing my praises because I'll always stand in your defense. I've overcome the world for you. Apply it to this and live a peaceful life.

Just as David prophesied, I'll vindicate you against the real enemy of your soul. I'll save and deliver you from all who pursue you, but only if you refuse to take matters into your own hands. You must refuse to touch my anointed ones, the ones I love and died for. Leave it to me. Put away all the harsh words, gossip or attempts to vindicate yourself. Just leave the whole matter in my hands, be kind and make room for my judgment. If you do, you'll find that I'll come storming in and cause your real enemy to fall into the pit that was dug for you.

Who are you convinced you have forgiven, but still think about in a negative way? Stop and think. It's an important question that I'm asking.

The old adage, "I can forgive, but I can never forget," isn't found in My Word. It just isn't there because it's not how things operate in the life of a believer.

Take the advice of David. Check yourself with Me as your Judge before you judge anyone else. And if you can't pray for them with compassion and a heart that desires salvation and good things to come upon them, you haven't forgiven at all. Sounds like a tall order doesn't it? It's not really, when you just choose to forgive them for the plain and simple reason that it's My will. Together we can get you to a place of freedom and change your whole life. Will you trust Me? Let Me show you who still needs your forgiveness. Relax. You're on your way to better health and an unshakable mind if you heed My advice. Selah.

EIGHT

Big Trials Come Crashing Down

– Psalm 8 –

In **Psalm 8 David** rewinds to his experience with Goliath as a child. Since no one else could muster up the courage to put an end to the assaults and intimidation of a filthy, foulmouthed giant of a Philistine, David called out to Me for the courage to bring him down. I filled him with the power to stand in the face of fear and confront him. Right there, Goliath and all his insults and mockery met their match. All the intimidation, fear tactics and affronts plunged to their death along with Goliath.

At long last, the "Champion" was disgraced and both the Philistines and the Israelites had a front -row seat to the power I can instill in the weak. The Philistines ran for their lives, as the Israelites stood in shock, barely able to comprehend what had happened. I "happened" and David never forgot it.

Many years later, David reflected on that great battle and wrote Psalm 8. He entitled it "The Death of a Champion," but all who were there and everyone who read about that incident can surely agree with David that I am called majestic and excellent because of what I do. I transform everything horrible into "Excellence."

David gives Me praise as he reflects on the victory of his past.

Psalm 8:1 says, "O Lord, how excellent is your name in all the earth."

Then he asks humbly in Psalm 8:4, "What is man that you should be mindful of him or the son of man that you care for him?"

Even though David was a child when the incident with Goliath occurred, he knew enough to realize that something had to be done because everyone else was paralyzed with fear. They were intimidated by the enormity of what they were facing, but David took a chance and the payoff was huge. I equipped him, defended him, saved his life and gave him an indication of my power.

That incident set his faith in motion to believe for great things from that point forward. It changed his life!

From then on, he could stand on his own testimony of My great and "excellent" ways. Of course, I was mindful of him. I spared his life. I've spared your life too. My hands of protection have caused intimidating forces against you to crash in defeat all around you many times. You're not always aware of all that comes against you, but I've hidden you from the power of the enemy in the cleft of the Rock. I've done it since you were a child and I'll continue until I call you home. You should have been dead already, but I saved you for a reason.

If you use what I've done for you as a testimony to My greatness, and remember the many times I've come to your aid, your faith will arise when trouble confronts you. When fear attempts to grip you, your own personal testimony of My excellence will be all you need to see you through.

Goliath was rotten in his grave and David was still giving Me praise over his victory. I've told you not to keep a record of wrongs in the book of Corinthians because I want you to keep records of all that's right!

Here's the secret to David's faith. He had a habit of reflecting on his victories over and over again and you should too. He could confidently give Me praise and call My Name "Excellent" in the beginning and end of this Psalm because of his good habit of pulling up a testimony of victory in the midst of trouble.

Try it. Let My Spirit remind you of good and excellent things!

My name isn't always rightly acknowledged in all the earth. Many have placed all sorts of gods and idols on the throne of their hearts that I should occupy. Don't be among that number.

Even those who have proclaimed Me as Lord and Savior often conclude that the Goliaths, those big, powerful and threatening giants in their lives are too powerful for Me to defeat. They soon find themselves resorting to the wisdom of the world to solve their problems. You know it's futile, so why bother?

I ask you now in light of your personal trouble and pain. Is there anything too hard for Me to accomplish in your life?

You might say, "Of course not, Lord," but I'm asking the question in light of those unpaid bills that are piling up, that situation with your health, your estranged or rebellious children that seem to be so far off, the brokenness of your marriage, the things that happened long ago that altered your life and yes, even that addiction that just won't let go of you.

Stop and think about what I'm asking. Do you really believe that there is nothing too hard for Me to accomplish for you? Selah.

I want you to know that nothing exists in your life that can withstand the power of My love for you. I care about what's going on and I'll rise off My throne to bring victory to your life.

If you come to Me with the innocence of a child and throw off your earthly armor as David did, your sling shot will become a weapon of mass destruction too. And just as Goliath's intimidating power was defeated by a small and insignificant youth, your weakness will defeat everything that stands in your way.

Let the mockers mock as they did with David and learn to refuse all temptation to think the thoughts of the weak. They rely on their own strength and will. You are mine and need nothing but Me. Shed your worldly armor and clothe yourself with the promises of My Word. That's all the armor and weaponry you need.

My Salvation benefits are so much more than escaping hell. They're a true defense against all fear, intimidation and strong forces against you.

Let those of little faith cower and run for cover as you stand strong in My promises. Be confident, dig your spiritual heels in and stand! My promises won't be compromised in your life. I always empower the weak when they ask Me to.

You may feel weak and even appear that way to the world around you, but use that weakness for your benefit. I know sometimes you just don't think you're going to make it, but you absolutely will. In times when you find yourself slipping into doubt, think of Moses, the fragile baby that floated into Pharaoh's daughter's arms. Fragile yes, but he was predestined to lead My people in power to freedom. What about Me? Didn't I appear weak when I was wrapped in the flesh of an infant? You know the outcome of My story. I went on to redeem the world!

There was victory potential stored in David, Moses, and the list goes on. What you need to know is that there's great victory potential locked up in you that's reserved for special "Goliath" moments. It's waiting to be unleashed at the perfect time. It's already been deposited at your conversion. It's in there lying dormant and you're bursting with potential. Come to Me weak and win!

Each humble step you take towards Me releases more of what you want and need. I won't disappoint you. The Goliaths in your life will crash in defeat and you'll bring down the strongman of your life through the very thing that Goliath mocked.

Listen to Me, no matter what fear, sickness, anxiety or lack in your life, it will all collapse as you seek Me and remember what I have done in the past. That's what this Psalm is all about.

Take a chance and humble yourself. It will be a terrible day for your enemy. Go ahead. Celebrate your weakness. What's your biggest and most ongoing battle in your life? David took off the armor that the others told him to wear before his battle with Goliath. Do you think with My help you can shed the clumsy and useless armor you have been dressed in for so long?

Your human attempts just aren't working. Try talking to Me about it. Don't say what you think I want to hear. Listen for My Most Holy Spirit that is within you to direct your thoughts and words now. My Spirit knows just what to say and how to intervene for you right now. Selah.

I have the answer. Goliath is going down... rest in that. Sit with Me and let My truth enter.

NINE

Let Me Show You the Solution

– Psalm 9 –

David **was a man** of complexity. He was not only a king, but also a prophet. As you read through Psalm 9, you'll notice a holy prophecy emerging and hints of the end times beginning to take form.

This Psalm reflects not only the struggles of David personally, but also the trials of nations. It can and should be declared personally over yourself as well as corporately on behalf of the nations.

Notice here and learn from David to praise Me in advance. He gave Me praise even before he made his request. What a beautiful aroma in My nostrils to savor the prayer of a faithful believer who is so confident that I will stand by My Word, that he can thank Me in advance.

Look at what he says in Psalm 9:1-2, "I will praise you O' Lord, with all my heart, I will tell of all your wonders. I will be glad and rejoice in You; I will sing praise to your Name O' Most High."

David was My prophet, an earthly king and surely a man after My own heart. Here he speaks of the end times as much as his everyday trial. To miss the depth of this Psalm and all it signifies for the future would be a travesty because it's a great source of joy and a blessed assurance for all eternity.

An understanding of what I say to you will cause you to anticipate the expected end with a confidence that can't be diminished. Hope is found within Psalm 9. The "Lawless One" will be defeated. He and all of his cohorts will be swallowed up in victory. Claim that for your personal situations as well as over all the evil that tries to contend with your country.

If you dedicate some time to Me and My word, you'll see that I often speak of the end times to you personally as well. I really want to give you a glimpse and even a vision of the outcome of your trials and troubles. Can you hear Me? Will you allow Me to speak?

Time after time, I've tried to reveal the end of your present sorrows and trials. Give Me permission to show you the end of your troublesome situations. Time spent with Me will always result in revelation. I have secrets I want to share with you. I have answers and strategies for you to embrace.

Time spent with Me lifts the curtain, reveals the truth, and clears the confusion. Time with Me is your only hope.

My revelation and strategies are so vivid and compelling that you'll begin to praise Me without reservation in the midst of your hardship. Why? Because the vision I show you is reality. It is what will transpire… you have My Word.

Let Me give you a good indication of what will happen and how the victory will play out. Which area of your life should we start with? There won't be any need or reason for you to reserve your praise because I'll take you to a place of vision and promise you won't be able to deny. I've authored a plan and embedded it into My Word right down to the smallest detail. Time spent in My word is the stage for revelation.

Come and see all that's in store for you. I have plans for a joyous and victorious life. That thing that you are hoping for—it's My idea and I'm going to bring it to pass. Speak it into existence with Me so I can release it.

Those deep waters will never overtake you and I'll cause you to come with unbridled praise in the midst of your most fearsome times! Ask for a vision and a promise to stand on and finally rid yourself of all fear.

It's impossible to be anxious when I've revealed my truth and the victorious end of your trouble and fear.

You can praise Me with your whole heart without calculation. Praise Me as if the trouble has departed already. Come to the place of triumph. See the victory played out before your very eyes. I know the end, I know the way and I want to show you.

Will you receive My invitation to set yourself in the midst of victory? Sing your praises unto Me as if it were over because it is! Celebrate with Me. I have nothing to add to the victory. "It is finished."

Don't praise Me standing on a platform of tradition and ritual. Shut the mechanics down and release your praise. Try it right now. I'll help you.

Uninhibited praise can only come from a heart that's witnessed the end of the trial. Here's the key! Follow Me deep and far, right to the very end of your situation. If you stand on my promise found in My Word it will predict the future.

Let Me show you my solution. I've already said, "Yes and amen." Yes, yes, yes!

Ask Me and I'll be glad to show you the vision of triumph for each and every one of your cares. Does this sound too good to be true. Visions aren't reserved for the elite. They're given to anyone who asks for them. Go ahead. Ask. And I'll show you great and unsearchable things!

Then you can truly praise Me. There's a difference between the praise you offer trying to convince both of us that everything is going to be alright from true praise that springs from a heart that knows the victory deal is sealed. Then your praise will be like the shouts of joy we'll sing together when I come for My bride on the last day. Praise Me because I am the same Messiah and Savior over your present circumstances that I am over the Last Day. I stand as Savior and Lord over it all for you. I love you.

In the end, when I come in My glory, all your enemies will fall and perish and we will live eternally together in joy and peace. But why wait? The situation you're facing right now that has saturated you with tears can be turned into a source of confident expectation. I hear your call concerning that wayward child, that lonesome marriage, that addiction and even that paralyzing guilt. It's caused you to look to Me and it's in My hands now. Whatever it is, I have it.

Allow Me to prove My love for you. Watch and see if I don't exchange your despair for joy. I will turn that ash heap you're in into a place of beauty. It all changes in My presence! Peace in all situations is your inheritance

Take a look at the end of your trouble with Me today. It will make all the difference. Is there something that's starting to seem hopeless to you because you've lived with it for what seems to be way too long?

I know the wait has been agonizing for you at times. I want you to know that I don't get any pleasure in causing you to wait. You've never asked Me what the end will look like. It's a glorious and triumphant victory!

I can show you an inward picture of the victory. Come and see. The wait doesn't have to be painful. As a matter of fact, it can be filled with joy!

TEN

The Potential of a Broken Heart

– Psalm 10 –

Psalm 9 and 10 are linked together. They both speak of the personal condition of David as an individual, as well as the surrounding circumstances of My nation Israel. David was a man of complexity. He was not only a king, but also a prophet. As you read through Psalm 9, you'll notice a holy prophecy emerging, and hints of the end times beginning to take form.

The "ruler" that you read about in Psalm 10 that comes from the "sea" of the population of mankind, will make his entrance along with the emergence of the "false prophet." Both will be sent directly from the Devil in a last ditch effort to influence many with double talk and all kinds of evil persuasion.

It's the danger of the evil that lurked from within that troubled David the most in this Psalm. He dealt with the disappointments and betrayal by those close to him all his life, but he was given a glimpse of how his dilemma with betrayal would be taken to catastrophic levels in the end times. And to make matters worse, David couldn't understand how I appear to be silent in such troublesome times.

He came to Me with the age old question of why the wicked are permitted to prosper and why I "hide" Myself when the enemy seems to come right into the courts of the sanctuary.

Let Me assure you, just because I appear far off doesn't mean that I am. You know Me better than that, don't you?

Take a look at Psalm 10.

Verse 1says, "Why, Lord, do you stand afar off? Why do you hide in times of trouble?"

And in verse 17 David cries, "You hear, O, Lord the desire of the afflicted; you encourage them and you listen to their cry."

Come here for a while and learn something important today. I have something to say to you. I can see perfectly. I'm not blind to everything that's caused you pain through-out your life and I don't hide in times of trouble. I see deep into the recesses of who you are and I know full well what troubles you.

You see, I know you and the extent of all that weighs so heavy on your heart. It hurts Me to see you fearful and anxious. I know how deeply troubled and disappointed you are. I know how alone you feel sometimes. I long for that void within you to be filled with My love for you.

You matter to Me and so does the pain that's within your heart. My collection of the tears you've shed are the driv-ing force for Me to come to you today with this message of hope. The pain that's been brought upon you by those you love the most in this world has caused you sorrow. I know the pain of betrayal. I am the "Man of Sorrow" and I understand. There are no words to describe the depth and pain from the wounds caused by someone you love. They were supposed to love you and didn't. They were supposed to take care of you and didn't. They weren't supposed to turn on you that way and yet out of nowhere they struck you down. The word "disappointment" now has a new and painful level of meaning.

You can be honest. I know you've even been disappointed in Me at times. You thought I wasn't there, didn't hear, didn't care. My precious One, not one thing concerning you has escaped My attention. Ever.

I've often bore your pain Myself and loved you through. You wouldn't have made it if I weren't there. I was shrouded, yet ever so present.

I know that much has been done to taint your expectations of others and now a fear of ever trusting again is sometimes very real. Your love has been great for others, your expectations basic and full of compassion and sometimes your tender love for them has equipped them with an instrument that's sharp and cutting and holds the potential to wound you deeply.

Your loved ones and those inside the inner circle you've created within your church body and friendships have access to areas of your soul that are vulnerable and easily wounded.

When you allow someone into these special areas of the heart, they can easily and even unconsciously abuse the privilege and cause your heart to break. And you find yourself asking Me, as David did, "Why do you stand far off, Lord, and hide in times of trouble?"

I know you've often wondered where I, your heavenly Father, have gone. You question why I sometimes seem so silent. I came to tell you today that it is impossible for Me to be at a distance. When you feel that way just come to a quiet place and you'll see that I haven't gone anywhere. I've been right beside you all the while. Your fear has blinded you to My loving presence.

When you love another deeply, you give that person entitlement and access to areas of your heart that are otherwise "off limits" to the world. You must realize that I am the Only One who can prepare the vulnerable area called the heart, for others to enter. Your heart is a special place, the seat of all emotions. I need to go there first and prepare it before anyone enters. I need to cover it with My love.

My love becomes a soothing and protective balm against all hurts and offenses. To allow others into an area where I am not present is dangerous and the cause of all sorts of physical, emotional and spiritual damage. Ask Me into all your relationships, even those in the future. Stop and do it right now. I'll gladly come and reside in that area and cause all of them to conform to My great plan for you.

When you love someone, you give them power and without my protection that power can often be used against you in ways that were never intended by that person.

Without My presence and protection of heart, the results can be a shutting down and an unwillingness to let others share your world, your joys and your sorrows. You know just what I mean. You don't need to push people away and forsake fellowship and intimacy with others. There's no need to protect yourself from future hurts. From now on, let Me go beforehand and pave the way. All that's needed is for Me to enter first and stand as your Protector and Shield.

Loneliness is the fruit of being wounded. A protective wall builds up and you go within yourself. When you invite Me into the hurts you've experienced, I'll begin to dismantle the walls of self-preservation that you erected around yourself. The power you've given to the ones that have harmed you will diminish and you won't be lonely anymore.

Let Me touch those wounds with My healing balm so you can live again. Let Me make it possible for you to love and fellowship in a new and different way. It is possible and I will bring it to pass. You have hope in Me.

When you let Me into these vulnerable areas of your heart, I neutralize people's power to harm you. There will be no more fear of having anyone enter your world. Friend or foe, it doesn't matter. I'm deep within your heart to sort it all out. I'll embody the good and bind up and render ineffective all the rest.

Suddenly, you'll become immune to hurt and offense. It's amazing what I can do with a broken heart. I'll even let you see things from My prospective. You can be fully assured that I will handle it "so the men of the earth will oppress you no more." This is part of My salvation package for you.

Connect with Me on a new level and join Me under the yoke I've fashioned just for you. You and I fit perfectly together. Man's sinful nature is no match for My love for you. I really am the antidote to all disappointment, hurts and wounds.

Whether someone has caused you harm deliberately or has just been too foolish to even realize the damage they have done, I'm still the Only Answer. So whether they boast about it, are unaware of it or have been remorseful, My love and allegiance to you remains.

Now let's go further. I want you to know that the hurt that others release into the world is oftentimes a case of deep and unresolved struggles and pain that you know nothing about. You are nothing more than an innocent bystander. And remember this: Many have been hurt by your blindness to the feelings of others as well.

Selah.

If I open your understanding of all the people that have been hurt by you, you would be amazed. Some are still hurting today. Pray for anyone you might have harmed and I'll go and heal their heart too. Take a minute and do it.

The solution to all this is the same no matter what the case may be. Time spent in My chamber, My dear child, washes away both the harm done to you and the harm done by you.

I'm your cleansing and healing balm. Restoration is still flowing from Calvary and has a direct path to your heart. I'm the Only One who can wipe away the scars and the marks that have been left behind from the hurtful things that have been done to you. I'm calling you to a deeper refreshing level. I AM all you need.

I do hear your cries and I have a burning desire to set you free right now if you'll allow it.

If I'm for you, who can be against you? Not even your self-sabotaging ways, which have caused the most damage in your life, can withstand the healing waters that flow into every area of your life.

Say, "Yes, please!" to My intervention to gently undo all your pain. I want to bring warmth and healing into every cold dark area of your soul. I want to bring you to a level of newness that you never thought possible. I am here right now to do it.

Let Me pour the warm oil of My Spirit upon you. I'll even give you more than you need. I'll give you an excessive measure to share with others. I'll cause a radiance in you that will heal and encourage others too. You have more than enough for I AM El Shaddai.

Freely I have given to you, so freely you can give. Here is your healed and peaceful heart, go ahead, take it.

My loved ones left Me in the most vulnerable and painful time of My life. And those I loved the most beat Me, spit in My face, ridiculed Me and finally crucified Me. I was desperately alone, but you have Me.

Won't you let Me help? When you keep Me at a distance. You're like a little child who cries for help but won't let anyone see the wound and tend to it. Let Me see. Uncover it and dress it with My love.

Apologies from your offender won't heal you. Anger won't heal you. Ignoring the pain won't heal you. Thinking about it over and over again won't heal you either. They just won't.

I know the area is tender. I am gentle and loving.

If you let Me see, it will be over. Just pause for a while and think about what I'm saying.

ELEVEN

A Clear Path of Escape

— Psalm 11 —

Psalm 11 takes place at a time when hostility against David was still rearing its ugly head. King Saul was infuriated. David had now married his daughter Michal and his son Jonathan continued his solid friendship with David. King Saul became even more enraged and determined to kill him. All this was just too much to handle for this insecure and prideful king, and David was in deep trouble because of it.

As King Saul's anger and resentment grew David longed to heed the advice of the unbelieving bystanders to escape from it all and "flee to the mountain." Although he weakened for a moment, David quickly came to his senses and began to focus on what he knew I would do—see him through victoriously to the very end.

David allowed Me to come into his fear and despair, and once again was strengthened by the truth that only I could bring.

When you are dealing with a crisis, are anxious or find yourself looking in the wrong direction for relief, don't run into the arms of something that will hold you in bondage.

Run to Me. Listen to your brother David and get your feet back on solid ground by trusting in Me. You have nothing to lose.

In Psalm 11:11, David strengthens his resolve and says, "In the Lord I take refuge, how then can you say, flee like a bird to the mountains?"

David wrote this Psalm after a time in his life when he had experienced countless victories, but he found himself contending with great crisis on every side. He was tempted to take the advice of the weaker in faith and seek relief wherever it could be found. But deep down, David knew there was no need to run away and seek an escape from all he was facing. He knew that I was right there with him and that I wouldn't allow him to be tempted or pressured to a breaking point. The waves of temptation would not overcome him.

I know the thought has crossed your mind, many times, to just run and get away from it all. And I know you long to escape from everything and everybody just to catch your breath and get some well-deserved relief.

As terrible as it was, I was in the midst of all David was going through. And I am here to comfort you and guide you through even the most troublesome of times.

Job's wife suggested that he curse Me and die, and some of little faith might be suggesting to you that faith in Me is futile, that you're a "Jesus freak" or using your faith to deny what's really going on. David was urged to "flee like a bird to the mountains" and there are many in your life that will suggest the same as your pressures mount.

The people that surrounded David didn't know Me the way he did. They couldn't understand how he was still holding on in faith when there was no evidence of victory in sight. But he knew Me, he had spent time with Me and he was convinced that I loved him and would see him through.

Are you convinced that I love you? Can you call things that are not, as though they are because of your faith in Me? If you have even a little faith, you can stay right where you are and hold on because no eye has seen nor ear heard, nor could anyone imagine the glory that is in store for you if you just trust in Me, your God.

Seeking ways of escape outside of Me is very popular these days. Many who cross your path will claim to have all the answers, but I'm here to tell you their advice is worldly and will not be enough to see you through. Carnal advice that doesn't line up with My Word will never achieve victory. There are ways in this world that may look and seem right, but in the end they will lead to ruin. Seemingly benign traps can cause people to walk right into the clutches of addictions, bitterness and even contempt for Me.

David was the target of malicious and spiteful lies. Saul's jealously became a vicious weapon against him and before long others joined him in his hatred and bombarded David with unfounded accusations and threats.

That's why David cried out to Me and, with shouts of frustration and fear, said, "For lo, the wicked bend their bows; they make ready their arrows upon the string that they might shoot at the upright at heart."

David wasn't going anywhere without Me and didn't fall prey to the easy way, which seems right. His trust in Me was the key to unlock his freedom. Simple trust caused Me to bring him up to a higher place, to My mountain of refuge.

My mountain is where David could rest and be assured that no weapon formed against him would succeed. From My mountaintop he could see from My perspective and view things from My point of view. To flee in any other direction without My permission would have been foolish and lead him into more trouble than his present situation.

In your hardest times, when things seem so out of hand that you think you will be crushed under the weight of it, I'll be right there with you to provide My way of escape. I'll lead, guide and direct you straight to the mountain of refuge that I've prepared especially for you. My place of refuge is a place of victory that I've planned at the door of the problem. Before any trouble reaches you, I promise a way of escape out of it all. My plan has already been devised and it's waiting with Me to be unfolded so you can escape the misery of going it alone.

There's no temptation or trial that will succeed in the "bending of their bow" against you. I've dealt victoriously with the exact same issue that you're facing in the lives of so many. I've dealt with what contended with them and I'll do the same for you. Now, their lives are filled with singing My praises and giving testimony of My faithfulness. That's your heritage too!

Any other way you attempt to seek relief is a pathetic attempt to escape your problems.

Abide in Me and you'll have true peace and won't need to add anything to it at all. Those things you seek to "appease your restlessness," the excessive eating, anger, perfectionism, closing your door to others who love you, and checking out of life, abusing drugs and alcohol, pornography and shopping. They're all ways of escape, but they're not My ways and won't work. How have they been working out for you so far?

None of them can help you and you know it. They call your name, supply false momentary relief and then leave you in the throes of guilt and condemnation. Is that what you want, or do you want freedom?

David described all pathetic substitutes for My freedom as "fleeing to the mountain." They're all means of self-preservation and are short-lived solutions. Sure, they'll give you a form of relief for a while, but be forewarned, they carry with them long-term consequences that won't only harm you, but all those around you. When you say "yes" to the temptation, you destroy a part of everyone who loves you. Why damage yourself and those you love? These ways are not of Me. I am the Only One who can offer you your freedom back.

I warn My people in My Word that "sorcery" would cause people to destroy themselves. Seeking anything but My truth as a way of escape is modern day "sorcery." I want to return you to the freedom and the potential you had as an infant.

I have a far better and more complete way than just mere survival. Stop circling around, and getting nowhere. Trade in your wrestling match with what tempts you and escape to freedom. Let Me once and for all, remove all the chaos from your body, mind and spirit, so I can reside there with you unchallenged and receiving the praise for the freedom I've imparted in you. That's total freedom. Selah.

To some My way of escape seems too easy, but that's My plan, an easy yoke for you. I want you to rise out of the ashes once and for all, to be released from the firm grip temptation has on you. I'll shut the mouths of all that call you to a place of darkness. If you want Me to just ask. It's a place that you love and then hate. It doesn't have to whip you around any longer. I take no delight in evil mind games. When I stand between you and the temptations of your life, they only have one recourse: to flee from you and scatter in seven directions. My presence causes it to shatter into irreparable pieces. You won't know where it went, but you will know it's gone forever. It won't be in your thoughts any more. It simply won't exist. That's the freedom I am offering you.

I can go to the place where you'll be tempted and meet you there if you want. I'll wait for you there. When you arrive, together we will claim My death and paralyze every cohort against you. With Me within you, everything will have to bow down and proclaim that I am Lord.

Remember that I sit high and exalted. Come and see things from My perspective. I want to show you My vision for the rest of your days. I long to provide you with a new inward picture of yourself! Can you see yourself in the Spirit really free? There's no good thing that will be withheld from you. It's for this complete and life changing freedom that you've been set free!

Do you want to know the exact moment in time when your struggle with temptation and fear was won? Do you remember when I was hanging there in agony and they lifted up a soaking wet sponge on a stick and offered it to Me? That sponge was saturated with myrrh, it was a drug used to numb pain. Myrrh was the narcotic of the time. Have you ever wondered why I rejected it even though it promised relief? The answer is simple: I refused a worldly source to numb My pain so I could offer total relief to you. Now My Spirit is available to empower you to refuse all worldly solutions that claim to numb your pain, I secured your peace by being nailed to the cross. Selah.

Stop a minute. It's all done. Receive all the freedom you need. Let that soak and saturate you now.

I'll never leave you or forget about you. When temptation knocks, I'll be right there with you. You will not be tempted beyond what you can bear. I'll see to it Myself!

David accused Me of being silent. I know it seems as though I'm silent sometimes when you're crying out to Me, but that's not the case at all. Reach for Me… really reach for Me… and the pathetic escapes that you've chosen won't be your portion any longer.

What have you used as your escape? What gives you temporary relief? What do you run to when your tired, bored, angry or just want to reward yourself?

Are you tired enough to come to Me? Have you reached the point where you know there's something better? Good! Then come, fill that void with my promises. I'll turn everything around and you'll never be the same.

Stop now and rest again in My peace.

When you choose Me, you choose the destruction of the lies that keep you coming back to things that will destroy you. When evil came near Moses, I told him to step aside and he watched while the ground opened up and his enemies were swallowed up in victory. No matter what you've done, when you turn to Me you become My righteous one. You are My precious child and will be protected. Watch as I swallow up everything that is not of Me in your life.

My invitation stands. Come as you are. Flee to My mountaintop and escape your heavy burdens. Continue this journey and I'll give you a taste of true, total and lasting freedom.

TWELVE

Refreshing and Powerful Truth

– Psalm 12 –

King David and the Prophet Elijah had something in common. They were both very concerned about the decline of morals among the people of Israel and solicited My help. They both realized that godly people were rapidly becoming extinct in their nation.

In 1 Kings 19:10 you'll find Elijah distraught and crying out to Me that my people had forgotten My covenant, were trampling My alters and killing the godly.

David had similar feelings and in Psalm 12, he too points out the scarcity of righteous men, reminds Me of My covenant promise to bless the godly and comforts himself with the confidence that judgment will eventually fall upon the wicked. Throughout the ages those who love Me have cried out for justice and have never been disappointed that they asked. Let Me tell you this. I am not a man. I can't lie. My covenant and promises for the godly will not be forgotten.

Read Psalm 12 with Me.

Psalm 12:8 says, "The wicked freely strut about when what is vile is honored among men."

My faithful remnant is calling out from the body of Christ in horror and dismay that wickedness, lies and deception are on the rise and that it's difficult to find godly people even amongst the ranks of My church.

But the truth of the matter is that some of those who are crying for a better world are partaking in the same evil themselves. They consider themselves among the community of believers, but fall short in so many areas of truth and purity. Many are finding the actions of others repulsive, but remember this: You can't pray against the evil of the wicked and then resort to it yourself.

There is such a need for deep abiding truth and although many are calling upon Me to move on behalf of their twisted and lost world, they're missing the point. My deep, life changing truth can't be etched upon a heart that casually fluctuates between truth and compromise. This type of double standard just won't cut through the levels of evil that are upon the world today. Purity is what I'm looking for, not dabbling in the same things the world resorts to.

The pews of My church are filled with all sorts of people that are conforming to vile things and there really isn't much distinction between them and the world. Evil is being said and done, even one believer to another, and the weapon of choice these days is often the many forms of social media.

It was bad enough when they used to just speak words of destruction directly to the person. Now their venom is available through the media for anyone who wants to eavesdrop and join in on the assault.

Popularity is the priority to strive for these days, and it's being sought at the expense of others who are put down in order to raise themselves up. It's bad for anyone who gets in the way of the climb to the top. Being accepted, not making any waves, and being tolerant to evil is something the world has come to expect. My people are complying instead of standing up for the truth. They read comments and make comments and continue on a vicious cycle that crowds out time with Me. What you focus on you will become.

The evil that streams through the channels of electronic communication is at disastrous levels and in an effort to "fit in" many believers are becoming part of the problem instead of the solution. Don't be among the ranks of those that gossip, judge or join in the madness in any way. If you want to belong to the faithful remnant, then use social media to speak truth and spread My Good News only.

I'm pleased with those who aren't caught in the web of this modern day deception and in keeping with the cry of David and Elijah, they're voicing their desperate plea for Me to move on behalf of the godly. They are recognizing the sad truth that society is influencing My people instead of them being the ones to influence their culture.

Purity and truth are what I'm looking for. Sadly, there's been a slow erosion of both throughout the world. People have become desensitized to the evil that surrounds them. Many are becoming just as polluted as the rest of the world and all because My truth has been reduced to what people want to hear and not what they need to hear.

The very first Psalm instructs you to seek Me daily and then meditate on My truth both day and night. Do you seek Me daily? Are you playing the harlot with every form of media that's out there? The entrance of My Word into your heart is the only thing that will cause you to become confident in what is right.

There is only a handful left among the crowds of believers who make a commitment to read My word daily and actually follow through. Pastors try their best to convince others that they should sit and read My word, but to no avail in the lives of so many.

You can live a godly life that's pleasing to Me if you will just read and study My Word. The life I promise is a life of freedom. I've set the life I lived on earth before you as an attainable example. This life is described in My Word to show you the way.

Become a person of truth! When you do, lies may circle around you, as they did with David, but they won't affect you. They'll lose their power over you. Let's work on imparting truth into your life. That's how you can change the world.

The godly cannot depend on the approval of others or be moved by their criticism. They are both based on the lie that the opinions of others matter. Only My opinion matters. The need for approval and the fear of criticism will erode your life of godliness and if you truly want to be a believer firmly established in truth, you won't have any need for either of them.

Do yourself and the world you pray for a favor and put all this far away from you. My Word should have the last thing to say on whether you are approved or not.

You'll know that I'm working in your life in the area of truthfulness when speaking even the simplest of lies repulses you. Let Me fashion a pure heart within you. Let Me bring it to your attention every time you tell a lie. Give Me permission to expose the untruthfulness of your soul.

This will break the cycle of lies in your life forever. Ask Me to cleanse your lips first and then the lips of the wicked. The lies that you wish to birth from your mouth and the lies against you will all go up in smoke!

Seek truth, My special one, I take no delight in a tongue that spews even the slightest lie. To exaggerate is to lie.

There's no need to color a story to make it more appealing. Simply let your "yes" be "yes" and your "no" be "no."

I especially want to remove the lies that spin around in your head. I'll bind the strongman in your thought life and take My rightful place among your thoughts if you want Me to. You can possess the same mind that I have if you want. Let Me renew your thought life! I'll impart truth. Then, there will be no more room for lies to feed your emotions. Truth paralyzes lies.

I know you're disturbed by the lies and deception that saturate your world and it is proof that you are mine in a special way as David and Elijah were. They cared and interceded on the world's behalf. Cry out to Me concerning the lies that people are speaking and believing, and I will hear from on High and cause things to change!

Even though the same evil of lying that was present during David's time still exist today, you have My Word that the truthful can call upon truth and will not be overcome by the wiles of any tongue. I shut the mouths of the lions for Daniel and I will shut them for you. Every lying tongue against you generating from the mouth of another or your thought life will have to drop their weapons against you. Whether done to you or by you, lies will lose their power.

My dear precious love, I want to pour out an extra measure of truth upon you. I'm blessed that you came to Me today. My truth is found on every page of My Word. The measure of My love is documented there.

I call out to you as you call out to Me. Come. Sit. Learn. My truth is at your disposal and it can and will change the world. Start with yourself!

Let's impart truth into your soul.

Are you willing to take Me up on My offer to cleanse you from all untruthfulness so you can then intercede for your dying world and the lies that plague it?

Let's "take the log out of your eye" first.

Give Me permission to cause a new sensitivity to any lies or exaggerating that you still overlook in your own life.

This will not only impact you, but also cause others to notice how refreshing My truth really is.

I need you to become truthful and speak truth into this dying world that we both love so much. Say "yes" and change the world!

THIRTEEN

The Removal of Exhausting Thoughts

– Psalm 13 –

Six verses was all it took for David to express his total weariness and desperation. It had been years of relentless pursuit for his life and there was no end in sight. King Saul was more determined than ever and David felt as if he was surely at the end of his rope. He just couldn't go on unless something changed. The thought of his enemies gloating over him was too much to handle, but his response to desperation was always to pour out his heart to Me. He was no stranger to the foot of My throne. His desperation brought him into My chamber and as he poured out his heart, I filled him with the hope he needed to go on.

Take notice of the progression of Psalm 13. David vented his emotions and held nothing back. He felt as if I had abandoned him and told Me so. He stated his case and revulsion at the thought of his enemy's victory. He felt My response to his cries were long overdue and he could do nothing else but release his frustration and hopelessness. He was too weary to put up a façade or paint on a happy face. He needed help.

David's honesty ushered in the full measure of hope he needed to go on. His transparency moved Me to remind him of a few things that day. In My arms, I assured him that this affliction and pain would reap a grand reward. We looked back at Samuel's prophecy over him together and I assured him that I hadn't changed my mind. I assured him he would not lose his life and one day he would sit upon the throne of Israel. I infused him with My Spirit of peace and all was well. His circumstance hadn't changed, but David did.

Let's look at Psalm 13:1 and 5. Psalm 13:1- "How long, O Lord? Will you forget me forever? How long will you hide your face from Me? How long must I wrestle with My thoughts and everyday have sorrow in my heart?"

Psalm 13:5- "But I trust in your unfailing love; my heart rejoices in your salvation."

David knew if he spent some time with Me that deliverance would come.

So many of My dear loved ones are crying out with the same cries of desperation. "How long, Lord?" They feel as if their hope is ebbing away and they are desperate for some sort of relief and hope just as David did.

David felt defeated and rightly so, his world was in turmoil and it was the hatred of others that caused it all. It's crushing to strive to do the right thing and have it all go up in smoke. David tried very hard in all areas of his life, only to find his efforts rewarded with trouble on every side, but his honest cries to Me changed his countenance. Peace is possible for those who look to Me. So learn from David and keep your prayers honest. Don't hold back, I love it when you tell Me how you feel.

After spending time together, it was impossible for him to feel defeated. A little time spent with Me did wonders for him. His hope returned and his strength was renewed.

I know you too have tasted the bitter pill of a relentless situation. You feel as if you prayed and prayed, but to no avail. Let Me tell you something that's important to remember always. I remember each and every one of your prayers. They are special to Me and I treasure and watch over them with My love.

Sometimes it seems as if your situation will never end. I'm reminding you today, of the truth that these long and unrelenting trials are not My will for your life. They have a definite end and I'm going to make them a platform for growth and reward that will come in a great and mighty way. Apply what I say to what constantly brings sorrow into your life. Stop and do it now before you forget. Selah.

I understand pain. I'm called a Man of Sorrows because I have encountered the heavy burdens and pain of this world first hand. Just like you, I've also experienced the wrenching sting of abandonment. The agony I felt in the Garden brought Me to a place emotionally that I called "at the point of death." I was so distraught that My body, mind and Spirit could do nothing else but pour out to Our Father. There was nothing else for Me to do at times in the Garden, but to let out a wail of desperation. And there's nothing else for you to do either.

When I arose from that prayer, I was filled with all I needed to face the agony of the cross. I became equipped because I gave it all to Father. I call you now to reap the benefits of believing in Me. I am making intercession for you. I'm pleading your case before our Father. He will listen, He will see you through.

I know you're tired of convincing yourself as well as others that it will be all right when you never see even the slightest glimmer of hope from My hand. It seems as if all you're holding on to is a blind promise and searching your heart to see if it's your own fault for the delay. My dear child, the timing of the release of your promise is perfect. It has been determined already. You are not missing one thing in life because of the delay. I have a plan and you can rest assured that I will restore everything that's been affected by the wait. Trust Me. The end of the pain will come.

Talk to Me. I understand. I'm here with you now. I'm here to help you. Selah.

Look around you, there's trouble everywhere, but the ones who put their trust in Me are in perfect peace and praising Me even before they see the results of their prayers. Why? Because I have filled them with My peace. Open up your heart now and let Me fill it.

Haven't I promised that I will lift you up and out of troubled waters? Haven't I promised to set you firmly on the Rock of My salvation and fill you with songs of praise and thanksgiving?

Is there anything too hard for Me?

Another thing to hold on to is that although others often disappoint you, I will not. No one loves you the way I do. As you study David's life, it will become obvious that things were often in an uproar and his family members were usually the ones who initiated it.

Saul was his father-in-law and hunted him down like an animal. Absalom, his beloved son, broke his heart with his attempts to dethrone him and many of his closest friends went right alone with Absalom's vicious plots. Betrayal can be devastating if you are alone in it. Most of My friends were asleep during My time of despair and the other one was out plotting My crucifixion.

Here's a word of advice: Don't expect too much from your loved ones and you won't be disappointed in them. Put your trust in Me where it belongs. If you don't expect anything from others there is little cause for disappointment. I want to be your all in all.

Desperation can cause thoughts to spin around in your head and wear you down. It can cause you to wrestle over and over again with thoughts of fear and anxiety just as it did with David. He cried. "How long must I wrestle with my thoughts and every day have sorrow in my heart?" As soon as he called out to Me I removed those thoughts. I gave him the garment of praise for his despair. You can see how he ends his Psalm with these words: "But I trust in your unfailing love. My heart rejoices in your salvation." He had a song in his heart! I put it there.

I want to be there with you when times of trouble come upon you. I want to meet you at the beginning of it all and carry you through to the end.

I have freedom for you. When I remove something there isn't a shred of evidence that it ever existed. That is why I can confidently promise you that you will look for the enemy of your thoughts and not be able to locate them any longer.

Don't continue to resort to your own ways. Has anything you've ever resorted to outside of Me ever put a song in your heart? The answer is "no." The only one who can put a song in your heart and joy in your spirit is Me. I am the remedy for all those fearful thoughts. I know just what to do to rid you of them and I will flush them all out of your life forever.

Give the truth of My Word a chance to help. All I need is a little time with you alone where I can instill My Word within you. Open your Bible and I'll direct you to the exact place that will minister to you.

Have a heart like David. Be candid with your feelings. Wrestle them with My Word.

And even though David frequently claimed that I was slow to act on his behalf, he still remained steadfast and pushed through. You have more in you than you think you do. You're stronger than you think you are and loved more than you can possibly imagine. Follow Me straight out of bondage to troublesome thoughts and into a place of song.

Give Me the time you spend thinking about your troublesome situations. Trade them in for some peace.

Allow Me into those times and you'll arise out of the ashes of desperation clothed in victory! I want to sing songs over you. They'll penetrate your heart and give you a new light and wonderful countenance.

So come with a humble heart and confess to Me that you're exhausted from all the thoughts that you struggle with and we'll take every one of them captive. I will contend with what contends with you and there will be nothing left to rob you of your peace ever again.

I'm glad you came to sit with Me for a while. Our special time is achieving great things for you!

What troublesome situation in your life seems to never end?

Now is a special time between you and Me. I'm here to listen to all that troubles you.

Can you trust Me with this? Who is it that troubles you the most? Selah.

Are you bringing them to Me each day and asking Me to bless everything concerning them? Do you think you have given them to Me totally? Why not try it again?

Place that person in My arms and pray for them. Bless them with every blessing you can think of. Ask Me to use you as an instrument of love to them. Ask Me to shine My Glory Light. It will flood out the darkness.

Spend some time thanking Me. You have been moved to a different place concerning these matters. I'm causing your heart to swell with confidence and peace.

It is well with you My beautiful one!

FOURTEEN

A Lifeline of Hope

– Psalm 14 –

From the very first sin committed by Adam, your world has become the seedbed for all sorts of corruption and each generation finds itself surrounded with all kinds of vile people eager to pass the baton of exploitation. David was so troubled by the actions of sinful men that he documented his concerns on two occasions in the book of Psalms.

His deep concerns for the human race is expressed in this Psalm and again in Psalm 53. Some call these Psalms "the twins" because his sentiments and fears for mankind are identical.

Fortunately, not every man is filled with dishonesty and the desire to do evil. There's still a strong faithful remnant that seek to live righteous lives. But, even the most upright person falls short of My glory and the abundant life I've designated for them. Even the most devout Christians, will find themselves sinning in one way or another. So regardless of whether we're talking about an entire corrupt nation or a singular sinful human being, the solution that David sought applies to all.

Throughout the ages the world has been dotted with My believers who've come to the right conclusion that I'm the only solution to their sinful world. David's Psalm passed the baton of intercession to many. Paul, the apostle, wrote the third chapter of Romans in order to depict the depravity of his times and to prick the consciences of future generations concerning their sinfulness and how it affects their world. His goal was to describe for all who read My Word, the need for Me to absolve the hearts and actions of all mankind and to continually cry out for mercy on behalf of the nations.

Paul actually quoted part of Psalm 14 in his letter to the Romans to show that the problems and ill morals of mankind saturate each and every culture and will continue throughout the ages. Where there are human beings, there will be depravity. But where there are intercessors, there will be mercy.

At the start of Psalm 14, David reflects on his own hurtful dealings with those around him. He begins with his experience with personal betrayal and the wickedness that's come upon him at the hands of Saul, Absalom and their band of followers. But as he continues, he comes to the conclusion that all this hatred and ingrained sin generates from the very substance of the evil one and that not only him, but everyone at one time or another are victims of it. He then begins to plead on behalf of the entire human race and their plight unless I do something to intervene.

I heard the cry of David and all who've asked for My mediation. He longed to see Salvation come out of Zion and it did. And the heart of the intercessors still moves Me to continually pour out My mercy and apply the work of the cross to the sins of mankind.

Read Psalm 14.

Psalm 14:7—"O' that Salvation for Israel would come out of Zion. When the Lord restores the fortune of His people, let Jacob rejoice and Israel be glad."

Israel was not and still isn't totally aware of what had happened in their land 2000 years ago. Out of Zion, out of Israel, I was presented to the world as an infant and changed the course of all people who were doomed without Me. Mankind was forging full steam ahead right into the very pits of hell, but their path was blocked by the plan of My Salvation, and now freedom from a dreadful eternity is a reality for all who will receive it.

David sent his prayer and cries unto Me as he stood in the midst of an unbelieving and perverse generation. As he described their corruption and captivity through tears of intercession, I surely heard his cry for Salvation for the nation of Israel. He longed for Me to send deliverance and his cry is the same as the godly today. Those who love Me seek My intervention and appeal to Me relentlessly on behalf of those who are still in the clutches of darkness. They are life changers, world changers and will surely reap the benefits.

I hear your cries that agree with the Psalm of David also. Throughout the ages, there's been a confident expectation that I will come and deliver My people from the wickedness that plagues the earth. I'm coming back, this time in glory, and all those who've recognized Me as the Savior that I surely am will live forever with Me. I've prepared a place that's filled with My Glory Light! It's spectacular and it's yours!

Cry out for those who don't revere Me and even for those who are lukewarm. Your prayers and intercession will cause them to escape the hell I've prepared for the demons that plague My people. Hell wasn't created for mankind. All mankind was made to dwell with Me. I'm moved by the prayers of My faithful so others can escape the consequences they've chosen. It isn't My desire to leave even one behind. You can still make it happen through diligent prayer.

Be a part of My faithful remnant that still cries out the Psalm of David. Let Me empower you with the words to say things that will soften even the hardest of hearts. I'll use you to cause sinners to fall to their knees and accept Me. Love others. Show them what it means to be truly loved. Your love will help them change their mind and escape hell.

It's all about My cleansing the world to create a people that are ready to enter the perfect world that awaits them. There's nothing that can't be forgiven.

I want to do a great and mighty work in you too. I've made it possible for the gravest of sins to be flushed out of your life by My love blood that was poured out for you. My cleansing blood still flows with power from Calvary right into that sinful area of your life. If you want, I'll continue to purify you and dilute your past to the point of nonexistence. I'm also here to stand between you and the seductive lure of sins of the future. The whole process is a continuum of purification that exists between you and Me. I know you want to be holy and I will make you holy.

My dear loved one, I'm personally tending to you to prepare you for the glorious Day when I'll return for you. It will be a time when you arise out of everything that plagues you. When I hear the command to "Go and get My Bride." I'll step forward into the earthly realm, find you, embrace you and carry you home. It will be the Day that you and I have been waiting for. All the times we met in your prayer time has been a courtship. Our relationship has deepened and I long to be with you in a more intimate way.

You may think that it will be a day when you, along with the masses of believers, will all assemble and be taken up in great numbers. That is true. I am coming for all who believe in Me, but you and I have something special and our meeting will not be where you stand in the crowd unnoticed. Each person who receives My glory on the last Day will feel as if they're the only one. It's because My heart has a special place for you that no one else can occupy. It's just for you.

There'll be an intimacy that day between you and I that you never, in your wildest dreams, could even imagine. We'll lock eyes and I'll look upon you as a bridegroom looks to his beautiful bride. No one else will matter. We'll have eyes only for each other. We'll captivate each other.

I'm coming for you dear one. I can't wait for the Day that you and I will dine together. Comfort yourself while you wait for Me and tell others that I love them. I'll come for you soon.

Do you really understand that when I return it will be a day of intimacy?

What do you think still needs purifying in your life?

What do you want Me to do for you? If you allow Me to touch that area, I will.

Relax…we're working on this together and you're doing just fine.

Let's continue to deepen our relationship. Sit with Me and let Me pour the warmth of My love over you. You are My true love.

FIFTEEN

A Warm Invitation Into His Chamber

– Psalm 15 –

In Psalm 15, David's first verse asks a very important question and the remainder of the Psalm answers it.

It's a powerful question though. It's a question that all the religions of the world still deliberate, but the answer is clear. It's getting My children to accept the answer that's the problem.

Here's what prompted David's question: King Saul and his son Jonathon had already died in battle and David at long last found himself on the throne of Israel. Samuel's prophecy over him as a young boy was now a reality and one of his first actions as king was to retrieve the Ark of the Covenant from captivity. He wanted to return It to Jerusalem so the city would become the worship center of Israel.

Inside the Ark, were the tablets that Moses received on Mt. Sinai inscribed with the Ten Commandments, a jar of Manna, Moses' brother Aaron's staff that was still budding and alive, and most importantly My Most Holy Presence.

King David's first attempt to bring My Presence back to Jerusalem had already failed. In his enthusiasm, he strayed from the direct protocol of transporting the Ark and instead of placing it on poles and carrying it on the shoulders of several Levite priests, he constructed a new cart for transportation. This was a total departure of the Law. It caused the death of Uzzah, and delayed the Ark's return to its rightful place.

His second attempt to retrieve the Ark observed the special laws and everyone celebrated as it was brought up from the house of Obed-Edom into the city of Jerusalem!

At the Arks arrival, David danced for joy! He and all his citizens were elated! He was king at last and My Presence was brought out of captivity and back where it belonged.

David was much more cautious in the handling of the Ark now and wanted to know the answer to his important question before he proceeded to direct the people. His question prompted the writing of Psalm 15. "Who may dwell in your sanctuary? Who may live in your Holy Hill? Good question, David!

It was such a good question that many asked Me the same question in New Testament times and I used Psalm 15 as the basis for My answer which is known as the "Sermon on the Mount."

Everyone wants to know the answer to David's question. They may phrase if differently, but their hearts desire is the same. It's a difficult question, but the answer is simple. Let's personalize it for you now.

Psalm 15:1 says, "Lord, who may dwell in your sanctuary? Who may live in on your holy Hill?

Throughout the ages, access to the Most Holy Place was blocked to common man. David's son Solomon built a temple and at that time, there were severe implications for any unauthorized entrance into My Most Holy Presence. There was a solid barrier and even a thick veil between Me and My loved ones and only the High Priest could enter in.

Even the High priest could only enter once a year to atone for the sins of the people and only after lengthy ceremonial washing. That's not the case any longer! You're on the other side of things. The day of My death on the cross was the pivotal point!

My choice to die and take on the punishment for the sins of mankind changed everything! Now each person can take their gravest sins and run into the pool of My blood of forgiveness. That's your ceremonial washing. You can come in! My love blood removes the stain of everything you've ever done wrong and makes you clean. What you and others deserved was put on Me. My death broke the barrier down, ripped the veil that separated us in two, and rolled out the red carpet for you, My dear believer. You are an invited guest in My Holy Household!

Everyone is guilty of sin and unworthy to come before My presence, but We wanted all to have access. We devise a plan for Me to absorb everyone's sins. It wasn't easy, but it's accomplished now. It's My gift to you. You can now come.

Here's an example. Long ago, not even Queen Esther was permitted to enter the presence of her husband, the king, unless he called for her and extended his royal golden scepter towards her. It was a sign of his permission for her to approach him. For the welfare of her nation, she approached him without him calling for her. No one just came into the king's presence. Esther risked her life. Fortunately, he extended his scepter towards her and she was welcomed into his royal chamber. The king was pleased with Esther as she stood before him and I am pleased whenever you stand before Me!

I'm waiting for you with My scepter raised and extended. Come, touch the tip and enter just as Queen Esther did. Enter the courts of your King!

Permission is granted for you to come into the holiest of places and yet you're not here as often as you should be. You often lag behind covered in guilt and feelings of unworthiness and you're letting your abundant life slip away. What sense does that make when I've told you that if you say yes to what I offer, you can freely enter?

You and I know that I had to die to make the way possible for you to enter. There was no other way. Do you believe Me when I say that, because of that great and terrible day on Calvary, your days can now be filled with wholeness and you too can enjoy My presence?

Do you really believe that My love blood flows over every sin you've ever committed and I flush them out and away from you forever? Can you see yourself adorned now with a new garment, that's spotless and radiant?

Are you rejecting the cloak of righteousness I've placed over you? There's nothing you could ever do that can withstand the power of My love for you. My love is enough. If you have to, read what I've just said again and allow it to saturate any lie you believe. Selah.

If you're still not convinced, examine yourself. Maybe you haven't applied My mercy and grace to what you've done.

At the Last Supper before My crucifixion, I had a great purpose for a statement I made in the presence of everyone who was there with Me. I said, "One of you will betray Me." Why do you think I allowed everyone to hear that instead of taking up the matter with My betrayer Judas privately? It was self-examining, a time for My followers to search their hearts. I needed them to think to themselves, "Could it be me? Where in my life am I capable of betraying my Lord?" It's humbling when you give yourself a heart-check, isn't it? Everyone in the room had to ask themselves all those important question.

When you get in the habit of searching your own heart, you recognize your own sinfulness, and as you bring them to Me, they are thrown into the sea of forgetfulness. You see, it's easy to detect the pride of Peter when he said, "I will lay down My life for you," but it's much more difficult to decipher it when the same pride pours out of your own heart.

All of the apostles had to stop and give an intense look into their own hearts. Big things were going to happen. Terrifying things. They needed to be ready with pure and humble hearts for the troublesome times that would surely face them during My crucifixion and resurrection.

James and John, the Sons of Thunder, needed to ask themselves if the same hearts that were willing to, "call down thunder from heaven" to consume a Samaritan village would fail and betray Me as well. Talk is cheap, but heart checks will let you know if you're the "clanging symbol" that Paul speaks about. They'll cause you to draw near to Me and receive forgiveness.

After Peter's "heart check," he did lay down his life for Me. His heart check happened when the cock crowed for the third time. He wept bitterly, but through those tears of repentance he was empowered like never before. John's heart check caused him to return to Samaria, the same place he wanted to destroy. Now after his heart check, he was ministering to them. Heart checks cause new and forgiven hearts and with them come newfound purpose in life.

No matter what you've done, it can be erased through an honest "heart check" and My love blood.

You soldiers, who've fought on behalf of your country, listen to Me. I know you're sometimes ridden with guilt and often paralyzed emotionally over taking the life of another person. I'm even aware that there was a level of satisfaction because of your training to defend your homeland. But now that you're away from the battlefield you think of things differently. Some of you even contemplate taking your own life to somehow even up the score. Let what I say go deep within your spirit and realize that what's being said here applies to you. I love you and Yes, you are forgiven. I'll wash you in My blood if you want Me to. The weight of taking someone else's life will crush you if you don't allow Me to help you. Your freedom from all of this is in My hand. Here, take it. Selah.

David asked Me. "Lord, who can be a guest in your house?" If you've never known it, hear Me loud and clear. You! You, My precious child, are welcome. You are invited. You are wanted in My Holy place.

I'm freshly extending My invitation to you today. I've been calling, but you didn't hear. I followed you when you ran in the other direction like Jonah. I saw you in the pigpen, on the abortion table, even the many times you resorted to alcohol and all kind of idols. I've heard every lie you've ever told and know of all your perverse thoughts. You've hurt yourself and others in painful ways and I'm still here. I still love you and always will. I'm not going anywhere and will pursue you forever.

For those of you who've already entered My Most Holy Presence and know Me personally, don't be foolish enough to think you've received all I have for you. Come as hungry as you did in the beginning.

With all that you know, you haven't even scratched the surface of My love.

The answer to David's question is simple: Who has permission to dwell in My sanctuary? You do.

Make your way into My chamber. Step over all the lies and thoughts that tell you it's too late for you or I could never forgive that. It's just not true, and I'm waiting for you. Wholeness is here. Peace is waiting. Let's do a heart check together. Take your time with Me now.

As things arise, I'll remove them. That's what I died for, to make you spotless. Come into My presence. My arms are open. There's nothing that can't be turned around.

SIXTEEN

AHH... True Refuge

– Psalm 16 –

Because of King Saul's insanity and unending jealously for David, the long hard road of fleeing from danger and death was an ever-present struggle in David's life. There were, however, two specific times when Saul did manage to control his rage and call off his pursuit of David for a while.

The only thing capable of stilling Saul's fury was David's refusal to take Saul's life even when I placed Saul in a position to be killed.

David wrote this Psalm during his "stay of execution" and he took the time to recommit himself into My hands because of it. Peter and Paul both mention a great deal of this Psalm in their writings of the New Testament because it contains a truth that's worthy of repetition. Psalm 16 foretells of My Resurrection and the hope that can be found in it. David was a great prophet of Mine. Enjoy his prophecy and stand on its assurance!

Why not read Psalm 16.

Psalm 16:1-2-"Keep me safe, O' God for in you I take refuge. I said to the Lord, 'You are my Lord; apart from You I can do nothing.'"

Psalm 16:7-8-"I will praise the Lord, who counsels me; even at night My heart instructs me. I have set the Lord always before me. Because He is at my right hand I will not be shaken."

Here is My precious David, once again reminding Me and himself that I am his Refuge and that he's safe within the borders of My care.

Look into Psalm 16 and experience David's declaration that's often referred to as a "michtam" in Hebrew or "golden." It's noted as "michtam" because I graciously opened David up to a golden revelation.

It's golden because it carried a truth for his present circumstance, but was also a revelation of the future for you. Psalm 16 speaks of My Resurrection. I gave it to you so you could rely on it when times seem to be hopeless. What is more hopeless than a dead body lying in its grave?

The truth of this Psalm is so significant that it should be engraved on your heart forever. It's your one and only hope, the hope that stands on the victory of My arising out of death's grip and coming to life. Sure, it speaks of David's brief reprieve from the wiles of Saul's pursuit, and even speaks of my Resurrection, but equally important, it's a clear prophecy of My great victory that is yet to come.

Psalm 16 is the prediction that My body would not be left in the grave nor would My flesh see corruption. It couldn't. And everything I promise hangs on the hinge of this truth.

The fact that My physical body didn't succumb to decay marks a clear distinction between Me and every other self-proclaimed god and prophet. They're all still in their graves and the bones in their tombs speak of their failure to defeat death. They all, no matter what they claimed to be, saw corruption.

All who serve Me serve a living God! The power of death has never had a hold over Me. And think about this: The same power that blew Me from death to life resides in you, Oh believer! And you will live forever with Me in Paradise, IF you are one of Mine.

You know I want to reveal my deepest thoughts to you and they're all yours if you continue to come to Me and ask for insight. I long to let you know My deep and unsearchable truths. Let Me fill you in on all you need to know about your present situations and encourage you with My great and mighty insight.

My insight will give you the hope you need to see you through and cause you to really long for My return. Come and sit with Me for a while each day. It's the place where hope is born.

You don't need to be a Rhode Scholar to understand great and mighty things. I've always revealed Myself to humble men and trusted them with my greatest secrets. Why not you?

David knew full well that any good he accomplished was first poured out in the form of a vision. Whether it was revealing strategies to win a fierce battle or showing him the way out of the grip of his torturous enemies, it was all disclosed in the secret place. He received the power of forgiveness to spare Saul's life after all the evil he imposed upon him just by spending some time with Me. My revelation released him from everything that held him down. We were true partners in life. He asked for revelation and I disclosed it. It was a great gift to David and I want you to have it too.

My dear child, why even think of going it alone? I've made Myself available for you whenever trouble is lurking. I know the way out.

How can I help you today? Is it a reality in your heart that I won't allow you to be shaken?

Selah. Stop and tell Me how I can help.

I want to give you knowledge that'll set you free. If you have a problem it's only difficult until you apply My truth to it. If you're struggling, you simply don't know enough about what My Word says about your situation. Not having a clear understanding of My Word is the foundation upon which all problems stand.

You can defeat anything with My Word.

My beloved Old Testament believers like David and the prophets longed for Me to come to them as Savior. They predicted the glorious day of My Resurrection. I gave them a vague insight into future events to give them hope, but look where you're standing. You're in a much better position to see all I've done. You're on the other side of My Resurrection and now you can more fully see My power and even hope in My return! You have My resurrection, don't waste the power it contains.

David reveals My promise to him in Psalm 16, and the apostle Paul resorts to the words of this psalm to instruct all who will listen. David received a promise that one of his descendants would always occupy the eternal throne. He was an earthly king, but I am the descendant Psalm 16 speaks of! I am Jesus your Lord and Savior and I will sit on the Throne forever!

You and I have the same Father and He raised Me from the dead as proof of victory over death. Don't be shaken! Read My Words and absorb them into your spirit. My miracles are yours to hold on to. What I've done for others is your portion too. Your freedom awaits you within its pages. Pick a miracle and stand on it!

The great works performed by the Apostles are documented for you to learn, so I can send the same power of My Holy Spirit into every facet of your life too. The apostles were no better than you; they just spent time with Me and believed.

My Word to you through the epistles, have been written to give you the counsel, instruction and the encouragement you need to live a victorious life. They're yours to embrace!

I've given you My Apocalyptic writings in the Book of Revelation, as a look into all the future holds for you and all who love Me.

I want you to know My Word and promises so well that they will automatically arise in your time of need. Out of your spirit will come peace and joy. Even while you sleep, My Word will counsel you. The knowledge of My truth will abort thoughts of despair, settle all inner conflicts and flow through you as a healing balm.

Know My truth as well as David did and let it counsel you in the night hours. Let your heart, which is filled with My Word, instruct you. My thoughts will become your thoughts as you read and absorb the truth. Your "heart can be glad and your tongue can rejoice" as David's did. You're secure within Me.

Do all of this and while you are asleep, a healing work will be done to rid your body of the tension and anxiety which claims the lives of so many. Set My Word before you and you'll never be shaken. I promise, that if you take the time to fill yourself with My Word, the power that emanates from it will arise whenever you need it. The cares of this world simply won't have the authority to snatch your abundant life away from you! Arise with Me in the power of My Resurrection!

What needs resurrection in your life? Take a moment and think about it. There's something within you that keeps you from enjoying life.

I can take things that are dead and give them new life. Are there relationships that need new life, financial situations, or how about your aching body? If I was raised from the dead there is surely hope for everything that troubles you.

When things seem hopeless, come; bring them to Me. Together we'll go to the Father. I'm seated right next to Him at His right hand, and I'll speak on your behalf as you say to Him what I said. "Father, into your hands I commend My Spirit"

We'll raise you up and out of the ashes of your situations. There's hope for you and apart from us you can do nothing.

Go ahead. Bring to Me your deepest hurts. Tell Me now because I am the Resurrection!

SEVENTEEN

Exiting the Agony

– Psalm 17 –

David's distress continues. He's exhausted, angry and ready to come before My throne to plead his innocence and appeal to Me to vindicate him against his enemies. He held nothing back and begged Me to act on his behalf. His relationship with Me during these trials was based on honesty and openness.

He was so sure of his innocence that he encouraged Me to initiate a full blown inquiry concerning his character. He invited Me to use my senses to come to a conclusion, use my eyes to probe his heart and My ears to hear his cries. He reminded Me that even though Saul and his band of cohorts had been relentless in their pursuit to kill him, he "kept himself from the ways of the violent" and chose to have Me determine Saul's future.

We both knew that he had many opportunities to take matters into his own hands and several of them would have resulted in a death blow to Saul. David was a man after My own heart because he was a man of honest and passionate prayer. He spent time with Me, confided in Me, and released his emotions where they were supposed to be released, at the foot of My throne. His character was birthed in My Presence.

We determined what type of man he would be and how he would react to the onslaughts of the enemy. He was vulnerable with Me and left My presence with his mind fixed and set on doing what was right. I empowered him because he came to Me. He was confident that he would be protected and that I would see him through. He was the "apple of My eye" and would always remain hidden under the shadow of My wings.

I cried out to our heavenly Father in the Garden with the same vulnerability. I know what it's like to wail in prayer before Our Father. You can be honest and bear your burdens before Me.

When you cry out to Me, I will hear you.

Why not read Psalm 17.

Psalm 17:1—Hear O Lord, my righteous plea; listen to My cry."

Psalm 17:7—"Show the wonder of your great love, you who save by your righteous right hand."

David continues to cry out to Me as he seeks vindication from all the onslaughts from his enemies. The heaviness of his burdens continued and his desperate cries reached My ears. His fear and pain where constant and there was no end in sight. He was asking Me to listen to his cry and hide him from the wiles of his enemies. He cries out and asks Me to "Rise up" and confront everyone who sought his life and to bring them down with the sword. He was crying out for relief from all those who were hunting him down and were surrounding him like hungry lions.

Their intents were evil and his trepidation was great. David knew that I would see him through! In spite of all his fear and anguish, his words of faith made their way to My throne. He was mine and I was his, and together we commanded victory over every facet of his troublesome life. He knew the secret to victory. He sought Me in all matters and gave me praise for the triumphs that would surely come.

I'm no respecter of persons. David isn't greater than you or a favorite child of Mine. I'll do the same for you. Many call Me the Alpha and the Omega. It's just a fancy way of saying I'm the Beginning and the End. I'm Alpha, the beginning, because I stand aware of danger before it surfaces. I am at the door of every circumstance. I keep a watchful eye on you and whenever troubles start to arise I'm right there to provide your solution. I am the Solution! I'm also your Omega, your victorious end. I have already gone before you and stand mightily at the end of your trials. I've done the work, paved the way and wait for you to arrive and join me in the victory. I've already pushed back the darkness. My Glory Light has led the way for you to meet Me in victory. I'm here at the end of all your situations waiting for you to arrive.

I've predestined you for greatness and anything you're experiencing that doesn't line up with my plan for your life will be destroyed. All things, all situations, all circumstances will work for your good. You won't regret your experiences no matter how painful. Why? Because I'll squeeze every drop of glory out, and we will sit together and laugh in the face of your enemy!

I want you to come deep into this 17th Psalm with Me because it has a surface meaning for David's personal life, but it will also give you a glimpse of what transpired on that dreadful night in the Garden of Gethsemane, where I was in agony on your behalf and poured out My heart as David did for the Father to intervene.

My hour had come. And although David was crying out to Me concerning the powerful devouring lions in his life, you can go deeper with Me into this psalm. I want to lift the veil of your understanding here. David's cry gives voice to My cry in the Garden. It's the prophetic message that is pouring out through David's Psalm. Stop and read Psalm 17.

I'm asking you...Who else could have really cried this prayer but Me? Can you see it now? Psalm 17 is My cry echoing through the prayer of David. Who else is truly righteous but Me? Who else could have stood before the Father but Me before I went to the cross? My blood gains access to Our Father now, but where would you be without Me?

When you enter the Throne Room, you're welcomed with open arms and you owe it all Me your Savior!

I began the greatest trial known to man that night in the Garden of Gethsemane. It was the beginning of the sorrows and pain that you will never fully understand. Your eternity was hanging in the balance and I made the way. You are My joy, that's how I endured it all.

So listen to the piercing cry of anguish and pain that resounded in the Garden that night. It cost Me My life so you can now come freely into The Father's embrace.

"Hear O' Lord, my righteous plea" was My cry that night!

The trial set before Me was so horrific that I pleaded with Father to find another way, but there was no other way, except to endure it. We would never allow that to happen. In the Garden of Gethsemane I saw everything that was going to happen. I knew I would be rejected by our Father so you could be accepted. At the thought of it, I began to sweat drops of blood. They were the first of many that would pour out of My broken body for you. I knew I would bleed until there was nothing left to give.

I saw everything that was going to happen and witnessed the events of the cross. The embedding of the crown of thorns into My head and the humiliation of being stripped naked before everyone. All so you would never have to suffer at the hands of someone who would try to humiliate you.

In a few hours, I knew they would shout, "Hail, King of the Jews!" I decided to allow them to mock Me so you would never have to feel the pain of mockery!

I saw the blood that would seep out of the stripes on My back so you could have freedom from all disease and sickness. Why don't you see whatever physical pain you have transferred on to My body. It will leave you if you do.

I saw the gash that would unleash the last of My blood and water from the thrust of a sword into My side. It would surely be finished then. That would be the last of it. It would drain the last bit of My love blood.

You would go free if I agreed to endure the Cross on your behalf. All for you My precious one... all for you!

Take advantage of My suffering. It was all done so you could be sheltered from the punishment that you deserve. The physical pain was horrific, but the worst pain was not having My Father to comfort Me. Our plan was that He would turn away from Me as I actually became the sin of mankind. Think of all the sins that infest the world. All of that was upon Me. I took the place of everyone. Now, Our Father can look at you and welcome you. You're not polluted with the sin that keeps you away from Him anymore.

My eyes saw what I knew all along needed to be done, and I did it. I made the way possible for all mankind to enter a heaven they didn't deserve. From the smallest lie to the darkest and most rebellious sin, the sacrifice of My life would appease Our hatred for everything that was evil.

I left the Garden with nothing but a determination to save you. My decision was made! Yes, I loved you enough. All the while, I kept you before My eyes. All I felt was compassion for you.

That's how I could remain silent. There was nothing to say. What could I say? Words were insignificant. My death would speak for itself. I'm your Savior. Don't think about anyone else but yourself right now. I did it for you.

My love for you held back the intervention of legions of angels that were ready to defend Me. You were worth the suffering. My love for you endured the crushing weight of all your sins. Oh, how I loved you then and love you now!

You surely have all you need in Me. We both know that you will continue to fall short of perfection. We want you to come anyway. You're clean and forgiven and loved. Come! Come often. Come in the Name of the one who died for you. The work's been done and the answer to all you ask in My Name is "Yes."

We, Father, Son and My Spirit have answered the cry of David and, "shown the wonder of Our great love."

Let Me show you more. I have great wonders of My love that are just for you. What sin in your life can you apply what I've said to?

Selah… stop and think about it.

Is all that I went through enough? Selah.

What do you want to say to Me that you've never been able to say before?

Now that I've shared with you, why don't you tell Me what you've been holding back. You're safe. I want you to tell Me. This is a special moment. Stay for a while.

EIGHTEEN

Everything You've Waited For

– Psalm 18 –

At long last! The mental anguish, fatigue and hunt for David's life was over. Saul's plans to torment David had collapsed and were put to shame. His years as a fugitive had come to an end, and elation and thanksgiving had taken the place of all the running, hiding and desperate cries to Me to spare his life.

David could hardly compose himself as his royal crown finally sat upon his head and Psalm 18 is a declaration of his long-awaited triumph. David purposed this outcome many years before. His sentiments are also written in 1 Samuel 22. He made a few revisions when he penned Psalm 18, but the only thing of significance that was changed was that I received greater honor as time elapsed. He was still giving Me the glory and honor and making sure everyone knew that he owed it all to Me.

You'll notice as you read that although he was now crowned king of Judah, he dubbed himself with a new title, "a servant of Jehovah." It was a self-imposed title that only meant something to him and Me, but oh how we enjoyed our times of celebration together. As He embraced the title of king, words of homage arose to My throne, and he hailed Me as his Strength, Fortress, Deliverer, Shield, Horn and High Tower. His life was now a testimony to My faithfulness and he counted it a great honor to be called My servant.

This Psalm came from a grateful heart that knew Me well, and even though David's emotions often plunged into the depths of despair, nothing could hold him there for long.

He trusted Me, believed in the promises that had been spoken, and followed hard after Me the entire time. The payoff was huge. His life was now a living verification of My greatness. He had the faith to believe anything now, and this Psalm was his way of documenting the great things that were done for him during his life.

You can't read Psalm 18 without noticing that, once again, a prophecy of My earthly stay is being foretold and described. David was called and empowered to thread glimpses of My life throughout his writings and this Psalm is no exception. My earthly life was based on trust in our Father, and through all the unfair treatment and pain, I too, sought the Father and triumphed over evil just as David did.

Read Psalm 18 often, place a bookmark highlight it, and base your life on the testimony of a king who refused to be beat. Read it when things seem impossible. It speaks of your destiny too.

Psalm 18: 4-6 "The cords of death entangled me. The torrents of destruction overwhelmed me, the cords of the grave coiled around me; the snares of death confronted me. In my distress I called out to the Lord, I cried to My God for Help. From His temple he heard my voice; my cry came before him into his ears."

In Psalm 18, David takes a trip down memory lane. He's on the other side of this terrible ordeal, but still reflects on all I did for him during those dark days as a fugitive. He calls to mind his cries of desperation as he ran for his life away from a fierce and jealous tyrant. King Saul and his army were a force to be reckoned with. They hunted David down like a wild animal. This long, and tormenting battle to escape death had taken its toll on him, but his long-awaited freedom from those who pursued him had finally come.

Now, at last, as he pens Psalm 18, he tastes the victory he anticipated for what seemed to be an eternity. As he reflects on those troublesome days, his attitude isn't one that demands an answer to the question, "Why me, Lord?" He had better things to do besides fall into the trap of self-pity. David reflected for one reason and that was to give Me the glory for seeing him through and sparing his life. He wanted others to receive the testimony of his victory to give them hope. The generations that followed have found that hope in his message and will continue until the Day of My return.

At the time of this writing, most of his enemies were dead and buried and the rest were bowing down at his feet. Peace had come at last. There was no longer a need for David to run for his life.

And if that weren't enough for him to live out his days in peace, My prophet, Nathan, appears on the scene with a solemn word that I would establish his throne Myself and it would last forever. He was enjoying the sweet payback time, the time when I vindicate My faithful ones and restore all that seemed to have been lost.

I was able to help him in his time of need because he refused to take matters into his own hands. He was afforded many opportunities to kill King Saul, but his determination to obey Me far outweighed his own desire to retaliate. His choice created the perfect environment for Me to move on his behalf in a powerful way. I heard him, spared his life, and brought glory and restored his kingdom.

As David reminisced about days gone by, a sweet aroma of the victory still lingered in his heart. At last, he was experiencing everything he prayed for, cried about, and even wrote down for the director of the musicians to play for Me. His long awaited victory was now a reality.

He documented the overwhelming fear and pain he felt during that terrible time in his life, but it was dedicated to Me as a wonderful testimony to My righteous anger and fury against evil.

Look, as he begins to describe how the very torrents of death surrounded him in verse 4, and how he could feel the chill of untimely death so close to him, it shook him to the core. He described his circumstance and likened them to "cords of death" or a chocking noose around his neck.

But you can count on My servant David to arise out of his fearful thoughts and proclaim the solid truth that resided in his heart. He couldn't go very long without having the thoughts of those troublesome days shift into another realm. He was a man of faith and suddenly in the middle of his thoughts, David remembered that I, his Lord and God, came to his rescue and dealt a deathblow to everything that confronted him.

He couldn't linger in the gory details for long. His pen soon headed in the direction of joy. What do you think his secret was? How could he stay above it all and not succumb to defeat? His thoughts were saturated in his faith in Me! His faith shifted his thoughts and moved him along a more peaceful path. That's what happens when you know who I am and recognize all I've accomplished on your behalf.

I want you to learn a lesson from My servant David. As you reminisce about days of trouble that could have easily claimed your life, follow David's example and turn your heartache about the past into an opportunity to recognize My love for you.

The cords of death that he described could circle around him, but they didn't possess the power to overtake him! And they have no power over you either. He had heard the recounting of Moses and the ferocious snakes that threatened the lives of so many in the wilderness many times, and he knew that if I did it for them, I would do it for him. He applied the testimony of what I did for others to his life and faith welled up within his soul!

The cords of death coiled around My people in the desert to bring untimely death into their camps. What did the Israelites do to ward off the grip of death that was upon them in the form of poisonous snakes? I instructed Moses to get a pole and attach an image of a serpent on it. All the Israelites had to do was look up and fix their eyes on the pole that had the image of sin, the snake, hanging on it. It was a foreshadow of My death. I became sin for you, and hung on the cross.

Go deep with Me and understand that Moses was showing the people that their sinfulness was dead. It was hanging there lifeless like a person would hang dead after being crucified. Now you have My cross to fix your eyes on. Your sin hung there with Me. My Holy Spirit will help you understand.

All those in the desert who were obedient and looked up, they were immediately delivered from the cords of death that tried to destroy them. David looked up! He cried out to Me and his deliverance sprang forth! You, My precious child, are also called to look up and receive your deliverance from the power of My Cross. Your sins were hung there to die with Me.

I heard David and the wandering lost Israelites, and I hear you as you cry out to Me. I will interrupt the gruesome thoughts of things of the past that try to plague you too. Your thoughts can shift as David's did and everything that plagues your mind and disturbs your peace will collapse and give way to what I have done for you in your times of trouble.

All you have to do is call unto Me, I am here to deliver you. Your voice is heard on High and I will arise and cause the earth to tremble in your defense. I become angry when anything comes against you. I'm a Consuming Fire and I'll be there to defend you! Don't be overtaken by your troublesome thoughts any longer. Invite Me in and I'll flush away the hurt and feelings of defeat.

You're not defeated. You are Mine!

I come with all My splendor and fury against the forces that would dare try and overcome you. I will leave nothing uncovered and turn over everything in its place to disclose the source of all that causes you grief. The foundations of the earth and the sea will be exposed to calm the storm in your mind. You can surely await My triumphant entrance into your situation to bring justice and peace.

I long to reach down and take hold of you as described in Psalm 18. There is no river too deep or fierce that will overtake you. I'll draw you out of the deep waters and set you high upon the Rock of My Salvation.

Your enemies are too powerful for you alone, but I'm here to rescue you. I am your God and Strong Tower. I'll pursue your enemies and overtake every one of them. My love for you is relentless and it's My pleasure to crush it all beneath your feet. They will not rise for a second time.

I'll show My unfailing kindness to you. I've set you apart and marked you for special attention. When you walk through life you bear My mark upon your body. You are declared Mine for the enemy to see.

All this I long to do for you, My precious child! You too will declare Me your Rock, Fortress, and Deliverer as David did. Look at the last verse of Psalm 18! It's your assurance that I will apply My unfailing love for you and rage against your enemies. It was promised to all of David's descendants and that includes you! All of Me belongs to you!

What seems to coil around you and cause you to fear?

Selah…stop and think about it.

Let Me help you. Talk to Me about it and anything that troubles you.

Your fears have had a place in your life for too long. I have the answer. Everything will be all right, so just rest and relax. It won't turn out the way you think it will. You have My word. I'll give you insight and calm your fears.

Look up! Look up to all I've done for you.

A refuge is a place where you can go to feel safe. I'm your Refuge. Let Me heal the broken pieces of your heart that fear has caused. Everything will be all right.

NINETEEN

A Grand Display of Victory

– Psalm 19 –

As **David handed this** Psalm over to the Chief Musician to be played for the people of Israel, he placed in the worship leader's hands a collection of thoughts that were birthed from his former days. He still marveled at My intervention in his life as a young man in the fields and later on as a hunted fugitive. His wonder of how I managed to turn things around for him when he found himself rejected by his son, Absalom, was fresh in his memory.

In those days he was so saddened when his lifetime of love towards Absalom resulted in a rebellion and coup against his kingship. How saddened he was in those days, but now as he presents his song of praise to the musician, his heart is filled with gladness for all I had done for him.

As he stood in hindsight, he equated My love and intervention to be greater and more magnificent than even the galaxies. The sun and moon, as spectacular as they are, simply couldn't compare to My loving intervention in his life.

He couldn't imagine going through life without My presence. Through this Psalm, he attempts to advise all who are pursuing a life of wickedness to reconsider their ways.

There's also a wealth of encouragement for the believer to continue to honor Me with all their hearts.

I've revealed Myself in the wonders of the creation to give you hope for change. David noticed My grand display of love and thanked Me for it. It's an exhibition of the highest form of love being played out in vivid color and vastness for all mankind. I created it all as a reminder of My greatness and power over the entire world. The unending beauty of My creation is a love letter to all mankind. It was written for the sole purpose that everyone should know that I am a God of great and unending love. No one deserves it. That's what makes it so beautiful! It's all about My causing the wonders of the universe to overwhelm you with My love.

Psalm 19 is a call for you to look around and find Me in all that beautifies the universe and thank Me for paying attention to even the smallest of details in creation and your life.

Psalm 19:1—"The heavens declare the glory of God, the skies proclaim your work. Day after day they pour forth speech, and night after night they display knowledge. There is no speech or language where their voice is not heard."

David spent many nights under the canopy of my heavens while tending his sheep in his early years. In adulthood, he escaped to the caves that hide him from his enemies, and many times at night I made sure My stars and galaxies confirmed that I was great and very much in control of his troublesome times.

Creation was all David had sometimes to confirm that his faith in Me was enough to see him through the perils of his life. By gazing at the stars, the moon and the sun as well as all creation, he was assured deep within his heart that I, the Creator of this beautiful world, loved him dearly.

I reassured him through the magnitude of the nighttime stars that even in the darkest times of his life, My Glory Light was all he needed to come out of his troubles in victory. If I could create this magnificent universe, what could limit My power concerning what troubles you?

"The heavens declare My glory and the skies proclaim the work of My hands," said David. He was right! Who, but Me, your Lord and your God, could create such a magnificent work? The universe has a voice and speaks into you the knowledge of My love by its very existence. My Word is true and My creation confirms it!

The voice of creation spoke to Noah as I flung a rainbow into the sky as a promise to never again flood the earth. I stopped the sun from setting for Joshua, and sent a cloud by day and a pillar of fire by night to guide My people Israel. All of creation belongs to Me and it's at My disposal to speak to my people.

Everything I declare in My Word is brought to life and affirmed by creation, so make sure you don't miss it. Put everything else down and drink in the love that's embracing you.

Illustrators are hired to bring children's books to life and their artistry creates a vivid reality of the author's words. More than words are needed to complete their understanding because of their finite minds. That's the way it is with you, the artistry of creation is used to fill in the gaps and your lack of understanding. I've gone to great lengths to illustrate My love for you, and My visual displays will add to your human understanding if you take the time to notice.

You need to understand who I am. Take the time to notice Me today. I want Scripture to overwhelm you! I want every Word to captivate you. What better way than to display its truth before your eyes in vibrant color and beauty? My Word has to be revealed in many ways or you just won't get it. The beauty of creation proves My point.

The entirety of creation points to who I am, what I can do, and my will for your life. There's a reason for hills and valleys, rivers and streams, sunsets and even the darkness of the night. I have a much grander motive than the purpose you see. The wonders of creation aren't displayed to entertain you. No, I've created all this to confirm My Word! It's a gift that brings Scripture alive and gives you a wonderful frame of reference.

There are all sorts of analogies hidden within my creation that validate what I say in My Word. Nature has a voice and I dictate what it says! No one can truly deny who I AM, not even the most skeptical unbeliever. Their attempts to reduce Me to the nonsense of popular thinking cannot withstand the voice of Nature that sings and hails My Name!

I stand un-refuted and will take all the glory when I return. Every knee will bow and all will declare that I am Lord and creator of all. Why wait until then! I long to empower your life now.

Look at the power and strength that My rivers and waterways reveal. Don't I often tell you about how I long to draw you out of the deep waters of your trouble? Aren't you blessed by knowing that you are truly like a tree planted by the side of the river so you can drink in all you ever need and want and be truly satisfied? Doesn't the forcefulness of the rivers speak? Didn't I swallow up every horse, chariot and rider against My people? Won't I do the same for you?

When you stand by an ocean, let it speak. Let the vastness of the waters upon the earth speak to you of My power to forgive you and truly forget about your sinfulness.

As your sin falls into the depths of the ocean, it becomes diluted beyond recognition by My forgiving and cleansing waters. A drop of sin into an ocean of love and your sins are no more! Neither you nor I can find them. They're not sitting on the ocean floor to be churned up by the currents of your guilty thoughts. I filled that sea up with the Water and Blood that flowed from My side on Calvary. Blood to forgive and Water to baptize you into freedom!

You're forgiven! Stop now and think about that.

Whatever you've done doesn't matter any longer. There's nothing you could ever do to cause Me to turn away from you. Let Me have your guilt and shame. Today's the day! It's your day of freedom. I have removed all that torturous sin and the repeated remorse and painful shame.

I've flushed it out and now I want to send a rushing wind over you to gently fill you with My Spirit. You're filled!

Selah…stop and think about what's happened because you came today.

Why do I describe Myself as the wind of nature that will blow wherever I want it to go? I use the wind as a narrative because you can't see the wind, but you can clearly see what it carries. You can't see My Spirit, but you know what I've accomplished in your life.

I allow you to be acutely aware of the power imparted into you. Didn't a forceful wind usher in My Power and affect My disciples for greatness on the day of Pentecost? The next time the wind blows, think of the power that swept through the upper room and changed ordinary and sinful men into powerhouses of My Glory. I desire to send that same wind in your direction. And then everything you say and do on My behalf will be backed up with signs and wonders.

When you realize how much I love you and have empowered you with everything you need, and I've saturated you with My peace, you won't want to sin any longer. Holiness will be your goal. Holiness will be your release and the relief you've been longing for. There's no wholeness without holiness, so forget it. It's my goodness that leads you to repentance and gives you the desire to turn your life around and live a holy life. Nothing else but My goodness will empower you. Holiness is liberation. Knowing how much I love you changes your desires and appetite. You'll desire to live a holy life and become hungry for things that augment your life instead of depleting it.

If you slip, I'll pour out My love. I'm here right now with a measure of power that I'm sending your way. Be filled. It'll make all the difference. I'm giving you the power that'll stir up the gifts you have within you. Wind, fire, water, the sun, the moon and all the rest of creation is used to deepen your understanding of Who I am and what I long to do for you.

I use the concept of fruit to explain the attributes of a life lived for me. I use the example of a harvest to teach you how vast and ripe your field is and how you'll reap what you haven't sown. My "Great Commission" is explained as you consider the harvest field of the unsaved.

How would you know all this unless the fundamentals of creation revealed it?

Look closer than you normally do at how I'm illustrating, illuminating and confirming Scripture! The birds and animals give Me glory by their very existence. Learn from their lives. I used the flowers to explain how they just sit there without a care in the world and yet I've dressed them in splendor and care for them. This isn't just a nice thought; this is your reality in Me.

Get up early and catch a glimpse of the sunrise! It's a prophecy of My return to earth for My Bride. The Sun bursts forth out of nowhere and appears shrouded in light just as I will on that glorious Day. Daybreak characterizes how I'll ultimately dispel all darkness and evil. The Sun foreshadows My Glory Light. Nothing will be hidden on the day of My return.

Study what I have laid out for you within My creation. It will give you a clear indication of how life should be lived. Be more aware of how My creation speaks. It's My love song that I sing over you. Take some time and let Me show you what creation is saying to you personally. The world won't fall apart while you break away to be loved by your Father.

What I long to reveal, the story I tell so vividly within My creation, is more valuable than all the gold and silver I've imbedded into the earth. To uncover a clear understanding of My Word is golden. Don't wait. Posture yourself for personal greatness as you take notice of all I've given you in nature. There's golden truth within it, and My gold makes a man truly rich! Go deep with Me and watch as nature backs up every word of it for you. Before My Word was written, I spoke through My creation!

I'm glad you came and spent some time with Me today. Something great was done in your spirit. Take what I've given you and look at creation with the new eyes I've blessed you with.

Now you know the true purpose of the beauty infused into creation.

I want you to know that you are My most wonderful creation of all. You are absolutely beautiful and you take My breath away. You have been bathed in My love today and nothing can change the fact that I am wild about you. Go in peace knowing that!

TWENTY

The Lifting of a Leader

– Psalm 20 –

David was a warrior king and the fact that Israel was always involved in some sort of conflict with other nations was the seedbed for Psalm 20. It was a cry out of the mouth of Israel for the success of their king and nation.

Psalm 20 was adopted as Israel's national anthem and soon became the song that was sung before every conflict and their prayer before every battle. As they sang this song, they placed their trust in Me from the beginning of the struggle and held on to My promises to see them through every battle.

David asked for "strength out of Zion." It was a strength he was quite familiar with. He asked for a supernatural strength straight from My powerful hand. David knew My power defied all worldly strategies and assured victory to Israel and anyone who called on My Name.

Psalm 20 declares unwavering confidence in Me and those I choose as leaders. Allow it to become your prayer for the nations.

David would often look past the obvious battles and would see Me fighting the greatest battle ever fought. It was all for you. I, your King, have succeeded and won every battle you find yourself in. Apply that to your life and circumstances today!

Use this Psalm to pray over all those who are embarking on a battle, including yourself. It will change things for the better. Don't trust in your own devices. Trust Me.

This was Israel's prayer for their king:

Psalm 20:1-2 "May the Lord answer you when you are in distress. May the Name of the God of Jacob protect you. May He send you help from the sanctuary and grant you support from Zion."

Psalm 20:7-"Some trust in chariots, and some in horses, but we will remember the Name of the Lord our God."

David was a man of war, and Israel was at war for most of his reign. The ravishes of war birthed this Psalm. War was a reality to them and still is in our time!

Many Christians stand in opposition to war and become objectors standing on the call of Jesus to be peacemakers. But their efforts would serve them well to pick up their Bibles and learn just what I have to say about war. I have called My people to stand up for what's right. And I call you to defend the rights that I died for. "It is for freedom that you have been set free." Now and always that freedom will come under attack and must always be defended. Let your resistance of what is evil be used as a sharp instrument in My hands to defeat wrong doing and plots to destroy the fabric of your nation.

I've declared that you should pray first for those in authority. Psalm 20 supplies you with all you need to pray and see results on the behalf of your leaders.

Many who never would have come to My throne are seeking Me for protection and peace as they find themselves dreading an impending war or terrorist attack. Teach them how to pray. You have all My requirements documented in My word and testimonies of great battles won on the behalf of the righteous. I've promised in My Word that when my precious ones look to me, they recognize the waywardness of their ways and are ashamed of the things they've done. I'll quickly come and heal their land. I long to heal your land. I make all things work for the good and many salvations are secured because My lost children have nowhere else to turn.

Get ready!

As times become even more difficult, people will look to you for answers. Let them find you at peace in the midst of the storm and equipped to give them the Good News!

Psalm 20 is the cry of the Israelites for their King. Your leaders need your prayers! Cry out for your nations officials!

David says, "May He give you the desires of your heart and make all your plans succeed." The Israelites expected Me to answer the prayers of their leader and prayed that his heart was close to Mine. Cry out that the desire of the heart that leads you is righteous before Me.

The Israelites speak of their confidence in Me and their assurance that I will bless the one anointed for the task of leading the nation to victory. They summoned help from My sanctuary and support from My abode. And they received it each and every time. Watch as I cause the foolish things of this world to confound the wise. As the days draw closer to My return, I'll cause your prayers to do the same damage that was done at the battle of Jericho! It is a cry for the defeat of the foe!

Pray that your leader has the wisdom to call out to Me as King Jehoshaphat did. Then watch as I cause every one of your nations enemies to destroy themselves.

Psalm 20 is a prayer for the success of the King!

Whether you are in agreement with your leaders or not, you must pray on their behalf. Pray for salvation. How else will it ever come about? Do you think the salvation of a leader is achieved through criticism or making him the target of your jokes? Your future is at stake because of his decision-making power, and I'll only hear the voice of the one who sheds complaints and judgments and offers up compassionate prayers for his soul. It's in your best interest that he knows Me intimately. Prayer and intercession is all I'll hear on the matter. So stop your judgments and lift him up before Me.

Psalm 20 told the king what type of official Israel wanted him to be. Never keep silent. Tell your officials what you expect from them even if you're the only one left to stand up and declare it! Never keep silent. The Israelites wanted a man of prayer to lead them. They wanted a man who would seek Me and plan his strategies of war in agreement with Me. Seek this also for your country.

Your country has come a long way from the nation it was when it called upon Me exclusively and My Name was revered throughout the land. As the Israelites trusted in their horses and chariots, I now find you are also trusting in the skill and devises of man. There was a time when I sent troops away from the battlefield instead of to the front lines, so there would be no doubt that it was Me who brought the victory. I used instruments that were unheard of. Praise, the blasts of trumpets and the marching of a few men became weapons of destruction.

Place your trust in Me and pray that your leaders emulate the prayers of the righteous king Jehoshaphat. He cried out, "We don't know what to do, but our eyes are fixed on you." Humility and trust equals power and the defeat of every enemy.

In your personal life, the battle is the same. Don't trust in human devices or physical help. I'm all you need. It's not a carnal help as in chariots and horses. It's spiritual help and it's yours on a global, national and personal level. I'm all you need.

What have you learned today? Do you see now that I am your answer on every level? Can you refrain from judgment of your elected officials and dedicate some time to actually do something constructive by praying on their behalf?

Prayer is the only weapon against the battles your nation contends with. It will cause strong men who fear My Name to rise up, win elections and defeat the agendas that destroy nations. Pray, lift them up to Me and I'll speak to them, no matter who they are!

TWENTY-ONE

You Were Created for Victory

– Psalm 21 –

Psalm 21 marks a national celebration honoring Israel's military victory under the leadership of My servant King David. Israel prayed as a nation in the prior Psalm for their king, and they reaped the benefits of their victory as a nation. The desires of their king's heart was a reality and there really was nothing left for them to do, but collectively celebrate and give thanks for all that was accomplished.

I blessed Israel with David, who was a true and godly King. Psalm 21 is his expression of thanksgiving on behalf of his nation. You see, the people of Israel previously brought their king before Me and prayed that I would send help from My sanctuary to him. They appealed to Me to make all his plans as their leader succeed. They put their trust in Me instead of in their horses, chariots and strategies of war and proceeded to lift David up with a confident expectation that I would give him his heart's desires for their nation.

Victory was theirs because they interceded for their king and trusted that I would see them through. All of this is just a nice history lesson unless you can see the deeper meaning and prophecy that I've embedded into this Psalm.

Sure, you are reading of Israel's earthly victory, but as you read, this entire Psalm will soon give way and bow down to the ultimate victory that I've won for all mankind.

Psalm 21 is a declaration of national victory, but more importantly, I've given you a foretaste of the future the ultimate End-Time victory. It's a message of hope and a glimpse of the triumph that's been won for you through My Death and Resurrection.

As you read Psalm 21, stand on the foundation of the testimony that I've laid for you here. Enjoy the victory that was won on behalf of Israel, but don't stop there. Remain on the continuum of hope that promises that I've already secured total victory in your personal life and also in the world to come.

Psalm 21:1-3-"O' Lord, the king rejoices in your strength. How great is his joy in the victories you gave! You have granted him the desire of his heart,"

Psalm 21:13-"You have granted Him the desire of his heart and have not withheld the desire of his heart."

Be exalted, O' Lord in your strength. We will sing and praise your might.

Just as the previous Psalm is Israel's cry for triumph over their enemy, Psalm 21 cries out shouts of praise for My answer. The war has ended, the enemy is defeated, and the entire nation celebrated the outcome. They asked, I answered, and all was well in the nation of Israel.

Israel sang a song to coronate King David and the same anthem is taken to a higher level as many believers attribute it to Me your King of Kings. It echoes a song that still fills the earth and will continue to resonate throughout the universe until the Day of My Return! Every minute that passes I bless someone with a victory. Why not you?

Psalm 21 was handed to the Chief Musician in the form of a song to commemorate Israel's victory, but it will remain on the lips of My believers with anticipation and expectation of that grand and glorious Day to come. Read Psalm 21 with new eyes and a light spirit because I'm right here to answer your call too!

All the people of Israel could do was give glory and heartfelt thanks for the victory they had asked for during their time of attack. They feared for their lives and I brought them to a place of victory beyond their wildest dreams. They didn't take their triumph over their enemy for granted. They brought Me the praises that were due My Name. They exalted Me to a new level because of My glorious victory on their behalf. They continued to celebrate their dominion over their enemy and you should too because I've already defeated them all for you.

Grab hold of the sequence of events here. They prayed, looked with confident expectation, and they received the desires of their heart. The entire land broke out in song and so will My Bride the church on the day I come for her. Don't forget I'm coming soon. I can't wait! We'll celebrate together! It's what we've both been longing for.

It's going to be wonderful, but for now, for just a little while longer, live in the victory I've won for you. Live the abundant life. It's what I want for you and you'll see that it's your heart's desire too!

David trusted Me and led his warriors to victory, and through My unfailing love, nothing could shake them. They were victorious and I was exalted. A winning combination!

My precious one, it gives Me great pleasure to give you the desires of your heart. I know what really moves you and how deep your desires are for things that are good, right and just. Underneath all the hardness of heart is a genuine longing for good. I know what fills you with joy and gives you deep satisfaction. I know because they are the very desires that I've placed within your heart when I created you.

Those things that you think are your idea were lovingly placed in your heart by Me along with everything you need to realize them. Before the foundations of the world were set in place, I instilled in you My purpose, My plans and a desire in you to long for the things I desire for you. It's all My idea.

I've equipped you with everything you need to fulfill our hearts desire. While you were in the womb, I downloaded everything you needed to accomplish all My plans for you. You were born at the perfect time, in the perfect place, placed into the family I chose for you. I've even given you the personality you need. You've been set up for greatness and predestined for the completion of My perfect plan.

You might feel as if you were an accident, unwanted and unloved. You might not know who your mother is or never met your father. You might have been the product of a rape, raised by someone else besides your parents, not treated right, abused or neglected. You might have gotten off to a rough start, but you have to trust Me when I tell you that your DNA was ordained by Me.

You were born to the parents that I wanted you to come from. It may not always look like it's so, but I knew just what I needed to create you and your earthly parents were an integral part of My plan. In some cases, you were the only good thing that was accomplished in their life. But, look what's come from them… you… beautiful you!

You are needed, you are wanted, you are valued. You are Mine.

The desires of your heart are intentional. They're deliberate and they must come to pass. I create all things with a Word, and My word was spoken to give you life. It cannot and will not return to Me void of what I sent it out to accomplish. You are predestined for greatness.

What you've done has no bearing on what I will accomplish. You might have run from Me the way Jonah did, but you were destined to come home to Me. Look at the examples of the sinfulness I've recorded in My Word to show you that what I desire for you will become your reality regardless of the paths you have chosen. I'll always guide you back. I'll cause all you have been through and done to work for your good. I need you for the accomplishment of My will for the world.

You are a necessary part of My grand plan, an integral part. Without you, something is lacking. I've sent many to tell you how important you are. Perhaps you didn't hear them so I'm telling you now that you are My precious child and nothing can separate you from the love I have for you. It belongs to you and you alone. No one else can claim it. It's a love specifically and intimately all yours.

Look closely at what David says in this Psalm: "You have granted him the desire of his heart and have not withheld the desire of his heart."

I've already granted you the desire of your heart; the deep things that you long for and I will not withhold those desires from you or stop until you receive them. You can expect it. I've secured it all for you on the Cross! Ask Me for the desires of your heart. Go ahead think big! You can't think bigger then My plans for you. They're great and lofty and they'll satisfy your heart.

You are postured for greatness, precious one. Start today to live out your dreams. Think big and pray them into existence. I am right here waiting for you to begin the next phase and I can assure you it will be far greater than the latter!

Long, long ago and deep within you, I placed a dream and plan that's been created for you and you alone. Certain things have caused you to stray a bit, or a lot, but you were created with My love and you're indestructible.

Stop struggling. Let the wheels that are always turning rest. Stop toiling. All your laboring can't add one thing to the blessings I have for you. My way is easy. You can accomplish things without all the worry, anxiety and striving.

Don't worry about others. They can't influence you unless you allow them to. They don't have the power to abort your dream. Stop giving them the power you give them. Bless them and love them. You love Me when you love them.

I'm here today to make all I've placed within you a reality. Sit with Me, tell Me all about your dreams and what you think is holding them back. I'll equip you each day with all you need to continue, and when you lay your head on the pillow each night, you and I will celebrate our victory. Selah.

Just like King David and the Israelites, a war has ended today, your war within, so let's celebrate!

TWENTY-TWO

The Link between Old and New

– Psalm 22 –

David wrote this Psalm in a time of utter misery and dejection. But as you read, be fully aware that you are surely on Holy Ground and that David is clearly articulating My suffering Passion and Resurrection for all.

David's plights and anguish clearly testify to My suffering in the Garden of Gethsemane. Because of My horrific death on the Cross, and the glory that continues to abound because of it, the world now has hope for a far better future in eternity. Because I chose to die and stood before our Father shrouded in the sins of the world, your sins, as well as those of the entire world are atoned for. The punishment came upon Me for you.

My death, along with all the pain and agony, is described in Psalm 22 and serves as a vivid description of all I went through. It's a link between My Old and New Testament. It speaks of David's trouble, but more importantly of Me, the Savior of the world. I am the Suffering Servant that the prophets and psalmists speak of in My Word. I am the hope of the Old Testament and the reality of that hope in the New Testament.

This is a very special Psalm, so approach it with an expectation to gain some insight into My agonizing death. As you read, you must know, My precious one, that I subjected Myself to all of it for you. You are worth it.

Notice the focus on the despair that approached David like vicious animals circling about him. His cry for relief has a deeper meaning than what you see on the surface. It refers to My cries of agony and the rejection that I experienced at the hands of sinful men.

You'll hear a description of My call for help to our Father and how the weight of the sins of the world kept Him silent and distant in My desperate time of need. All of these depictions in Psalm 22 have been documented in order for you to get a glimpse of what it cost Me to save you. It will also tie the entire content of My Word together for you to understand.

I called out to the Father as My very blood, breadth, and life were draining out of Me. I suffered the agony of our Father's rejection as I cried out to Him to assure you that He would always respond to yours. And We have placed a measure of faith in you that will help you call for Our help in your time of need.

David says in Psalm 22:9, "Yet you brought Me out of the womb, you made Me trust in you even at My mother's breasts."

David was right when he testified that I brought him out of the womb and caused him to trust in Me even as an infant, and the same holds true for you. From the time you emerged from the womb, to your present day, I've been an ever-present Father to you. You were presented at the moment of your birth into My loving arms where you will remain always. You were handed over and into the arms of some caring individual of course, but greater than that was My embrace that has never lost its loving hold upon your life.

It was one gentle motion out of the secret place of the womb and into My embrace. My watchful eye was upon you in the place where you were formed and I still keep watch over you and shelter you within My arms as a mother embraces her newborn.

Please don't look to another human being for the things that only I can give you because they'll always disappoint you. I'm your Heavenly Father. To look to your earthly father or mother, spouse or child for the deepest needs of your heart will never work. You're looking in the direction of a human being for something they're incapable of giving you. It's just Me and you... remember that always.

They don't know anything about the kind of love you need and it isn't theirs to give. I won't even allow the best of earthly fathers and mothers to love you the way I love you. Come to Me and receive the Fatherly love you long for.

Selah. Take a minute and allow Me to love you.

This beautiful relationship, which began even before your birth, was interrupted for a while by the evil in the world. There came a time of great interference, a time of your leaving Me for a while, when disappointments set in, when people treated you harshly or even when the sinfulness of your own heart lured you away. You wandered off and thought you left Me or that I left you. But I was right beside you making sure that you didn't go as far as you would have liked to. I erected a spiritual hedge of thorns that you couldn't see. It prevented you from getting to the evil you blindly approached. It was Me all the while making sure you didn't go to the point of total destruction. I've spared your life. You know that within your heart.

Because of the Cross, the blood that was shed in love will always draw you back into My arms. I will always call you by name and show you the way home. Sometimes, I have to pick you up out of the place your wrong decisions have taken you and carry you back where you belong. The same arms that embraced you at birth are the ones that hold you up and even long to receive you after you've strayed.

The day you came to Me and gave me your heart was truly a day of rebirth. You have no idea of the impact that your return made on you and the world. You were given a place in My kingdom and clothed with new garments that can never be stained again. I've washed them in My blood. Sinless blood is the only thing that could wash away all the years that you went your own way.

But you're back where you belong, and you're as pure as a newborn infant.

I knew you would come back. I planned for your return. I died so everything could be restored. The shackles that coil around you, the mental and emotional anguish, even the illnesses that try to cling to you have to let you go. The grip that holds you has to release you. You are Mine and set free.

I used David to utter truth to you. He was a prophet and spoke the very words that surrounded My death. Surely the horror that David speaks of far exceeds anything he had to endure. He speaks of a death by crucifixion, a type of death he knew nothing about except for my prophetic anointing upon his life. No one but Me your Messiah has ever been forsaken by our Father. No one experienced this type of horrific sorrow.

My cry, "My God, My God, why have you forsaken Me?" were words that expressed an exclusive sorrow that was inflicted solely upon Me for your freedom. The rest of the world is exempt from this pain and sorrow because I stood in their place.

When you read Psalm 22, look within it until you find Me. It was written so you would know what was done to win your freedom.

I've spoken of My deep and everlasting love for all mankind through My prophet. David and I speak to you now so you can know deep within your heart that I will never leave you. Let David remind you that I was there when you were developing in your mother's womb. I was there at your birth. I was there when you were going through the trials of your life. I cry with you when others hurt you. I've given people free will. I want you to understand that it grieves Me to see you hurting in any way. It wasn't Me who harmed you. I gave My life for you.

I offer you today a deep and inner healing for your spirit, body and mind. I long to heal all that has broken your heart... let Me do it.

Just sit with Me and let what I have said sink deeply into your spirit. We, Father, Son and Holy Spirit are here to heal you deeply.

Allow the deepest recesses of your heart to open up right now. It's all coming up and out. You are safe within My embrace and everything will be alright... Selah.

TWENTY-THREE

Your Cup Overflows

– Psalm 23 –

Look at this Psalm with sheer delight because that's how the writer felt when he wrote it. He's thankful and confident because he's lived a long life, and his reflection is filled with the awareness that I was and will always be there for him. David was an old man and one who experienced many mountaintop encounters and sunk low into the valley of despair. He was no stranger to the shadow of death, for it had confronted him on many occasions.

This Psalm is popular one because it resonates with the hearts of so many and describes how I always meet the needs of My beloved. All of the details listed in David's Psalm are quite familiar and common to all mankind.

The first portion portrays Me as his Shepherd, the latter part as Host of the greatest wedding feast of all times. It will be a banquet and victory celebration that will cause ultimate joy in the hearts of all believers and mock the enemy as he witnesses our triumph.

My gift to David was victory in both the important and even in the insignificant areas of his life. His cup overflowed with gladness to the point of spilling over.

Let Me fill yours today!

Psalm 23:5-" My cup overflows."

What a wonderful gift I've given you! It's a gift like none other! The word "Salvation" has become quite familiar hasn't it? You use the word "Salvation" to define the undeserved gift that awaits you at the end of your earthly life. And you're quite right about that.

You've grasped a good concept of My mercy and grace and have even come to the glorious conclusion that accepting My Words, Death, and Resurrection for your sins will cause you to spend eternity with Me in heaven. But you're sorely lacking the full scope of My love for you if you reduce My Salvation work to only your future. I have so much more for you than a ticket to heaven.

You see, My precious child, as spectacular as My 2nd coming is, and as wonderful as our spending eternity together may be, there's still so much more. The abundant and overwhelming plan I have for you can't be limited to one element of time. It can't be confined to what I will do for you. It has to be expressed right here and now and encompass all aspects of your life. It has to meet you where you are, then flow back to your past and on to your future.

Do you get what I'm offering you here? It's a life full of My provisions to meet your every need. It was created to heal your past, stand with you as you face your current life, and also give you hope for eternity. Make sure you receive all you're entitled to. It's a gift with salvation provisions for every dimension of your life!

My Salvation can be likened to a package or a gift basket. It doesn't contain just one gift; it contains many! My beautiful child, when you call yourself "saved" it means you've entered into a totally new existence. You don't have to wait for eternity to enjoy the benefits of My Salvation Package. Embrace its entirety now! That's how you taste and see that I am surely good.

I know you have needs that require tending to right now. I'm very much aware of what troubles you, and I want to help. Open the package! Take what you need! This gift cost Me My life and I want you to have it.

When you really understand what I'm saying and what I'm offering you, it will change your world! My love for you will take on another whole dimension, and then you can start to apply your gift to everything in your present life!

Every fear, every decision, every sorrow, all the heart-ache you have along with all your needs will receive a fresh infilling of solution and Love. All your disappointments and desires of your heart will truly be captivated and turned around to serve you and bring Me glory! That's how it works!

You will become surrounded with peace and joy no matter what's going on because My gift of your Salvation Package covers it all! All it takes is for you to understand My Love. And if that's not enough, here's the best part: No matter how much you're disappointed with yourself, hate the choices you've made, or even the person you've become, My offer to bless you with My Salvation Package still stands.

Let's talk about temptation. When you accept My free Salvation Package, you're no longer bound to your sinful nature. Your will power never worked for you anyway. All your striving and pretending and trying to hold out a little longer only empowered the temptation even more.

That was all a fleshly way to try and please Me and fight against something you're powerless to defeat on your own. Here's the truth: When you really come to know how much I love you, and when you slip your hand in Mine, the grip of temptation is forced to give you back to Me. The power that the temptation has over you is diminished. My Salvation Package includes a healthy dose of resistance, so your enemies will have to flee each and every time they attempt to bring you down. You'll have the strength to say no and mean it this time.

Precious one, I long to disclose My original purpose and the many gifts that have been kept at bay because of your lack of understanding. You think you know Me, but really, there's so much more of Me to be had. My love for you is inexhaustible. It's all encompassing! And I'm bursting with a desire to save you from all your circumstances. Won't you let the river of My love flow over your life?

My Salvation Package is relevant to what you're going through right at this very moment. If I asked you what your deepest sorrow is today, what would you say? Take a minute and think about what I just asked you. Where do you need help?

That's where I want to start!

I want to apply My Salvation Package right there and begin to unfurl My Glory Light over you! I want to flow back to areas that hurt and are causing you pain, immerse all the situations that are coiling around you today and pave your future with one loving solution after another.

They're all hungry lions. Let Me shut them up. Let Me soak your financial needs, your body, your will, your mind, your emotions and your memory with My salvation. Let Me save you from yourself. Selah.

David speaks of his cup overflowing. In order to overflow, a cup must have a continual supply that causes it to spill over in abundance. Your cup, which is your life and everything that has to do with you, must overflow with My grace, or there is no chance of true joy. Not one area of your life should be excluded.

What troubles you today? Let Me help. Let Me in.

I've made wonderful provisions for your weakness, your enemies and your future. Past, present and future are all taken care of. It's My Salvation Package!

The river of My love began to flow as drops of agony fell in the Garden of Gethsemane. Each crack of the whip against My back purchased your peace, healing, and every provision you will ever need. It's finished! The package is complete! Nothing else is needed except for you to call the flow of My Salvation down upon your life.

I want My salvation to flow into your life more than it is now. I don't want you sick, in debt or paralyzed by your past. You don't have to be afraid to face the future any longer and the past regrets are washed away.

My Love blood longs to flow into every one of your relationships too. You may think they've been torn into irreparable pieces, but they're not! All dividing walls and barriers to restoration will come down. I promise. Look to Me in hope. Ask Me to pour more peace into your life. I'm waiting. I did everything so I would have the pleasure of helping you live a life worth living.

Didn't I promise that I would not withhold any good thing from you? That includes your past, present and future in this dimension of life. It's yours, right here and right now. In order for Me to keep My promise, peace and solution has to pour over you now as well as in the future. You need healing in your body and the power to obtain wealth now. Reconciliation with a loved one doesn't have to wait. These are the things I need to work out for you and I'm perfectly capable.

The process needs to be started. Why wait?

I've told you that trouble will come, but it doesn't stand a chance when My salvation pours over it. I love you so much more than you think I do.

Perhaps you've heard people apply My blood to their situations. They are right to do so. They pray and "Plead the blood." Well you can plead all you want, but if you don't have a clear understanding of what you're doing, it will be futile.

Let Me explain. My blood still pours from Calvary. It has many components. Some of these components are protection, peace, healing, and many other expressions of My love. My relentless love for you is embodied in it. Blood always carries life. Human blood contains life-giving and life-supporting components. My love blood contains everything you'll ever need or want. When you use the word "plead," it's the same word that used in a court of law. So really, when you "plead" My blood you are using it as an argument against the devises of the enemy just as a lawyer would "plead" your case before a judge.

I instructed the Israelites to paint the sashes and doorposts of their homes with the blood of a lamb that was sacrificed. When they did, they were protected and life was spared because of the spiritual covering that the blood represented. I am the Lamb of God! When you pray that My blood covers you and your loved ones, protection is guaranteed! It's part of your Salvation Package!

In this Psalm, David uses the metaphor of a lamb and its shepherd. He depicts the assured life of an innocent lamb under the loving care of its watchman. He speaks of the confidence a lamb has as it lies down in green pastures. There's no fear, just absolute peace.

I've promised to make you lie down in green pastures too, but let Me ask you something. What exactly are your personal green pastures? Sheep need a place to graze and lie down to rest. Your needs are far greater than that, and I long to bed you down in your own green pastures. What ever they are to you is between you and Me. I can create a pasture that can cause everything concerning you to turn into a peaceful conclusion.

Is your green pasture financial stability or being brought out of the clutches of an addiction? Is your green pasture restoration of your mind? A healing in your body? What would put you at ease and make you feel as if you were lying in a peaceful green pasture? Could it be once and for all the silencing of all guilt and shame? Really, your green pasture would be to never have to think about that issue again.

What if the alcoholic never thought about alcohol again? That's the level of peace I want to bring into your life. That's the lush green pasture David speaks of. Whatever's disturbing you, I long to set you free from it today.

Selah.

When your loved ones have disappointed you so badly that you feel you will just be crushed by the weight of it, remember that I was crushed so you don't have to be. Right at the very moment when you feel as if you can't go on, My River will start to flow and bring with it the peace you need to get through. I won't let it overtake you!

I am here ready to fill your cup to overflowing. Let it spill over. Let the blood that poured out at Calvary flow now. There's nothing that can withstand the power of My love for you. Bring to Me the things that seem to have no end.

I know certain areas of your life have the power to over-whelm you at times, but here's the river of provision I've been telling you about. For a long time, you've been relying on your own strength to calm the storms and stamp out the fires. You were never made to carry it all. Trust Me in a way you never have before so I can help. My Holy Spirit is bringing up the area I want to take care of.

Linger with Me.

Now here! Accept your package of My gift of Salvation. Go ahead open it!

Selah.

TWENTY-FOUR

Your Chains Have Been Broken

– Psalm 24 –

This Psalm was written to commemorate My Ark of the Covenant's return to its homeland in Jerusalem! The people shouted this song in tribute to Me because I burned a hole right through the barriers the Philistines erected to hold My Ark in captivity. They took it. It was not theirs, and they could do nothing else but give it back. The ancient gates of captivity had to release My Ark to its rightful owners, My chosen people the Israelites.

The gates had to open up and give way! The everlasting doors had to be opened, for I, the King of Glory, was making My entry! The gatekeeper was commanded to step aside. I was taking My rightful position amongst My chosen people. The attempts of the Philistines were disgraced and defeated. And I made My triumphant entrance into My homeland! It was finished! My plan was being carried out and nothing could stop it.

Before its capture, the Ark of the Covenant accompanied My people and lead them in dramatic power. It was created to lead the Israelites, and My Presence displayed dramatic power on many occasions. Because of the presence of the Ark of the Covenant, the Jordan River was split for Joshua, and it also caused the walls of Jericho to crumble as the soldiers marched and offered up praise.

Eventually, the Philistines captured the Ark and they regretted every minute of it. They thought they could incarcerate My glory from the Israelites and decided to place it alongside their graven image and god Dagon. Too bad for them and Dagon! The power of My Presence caused their man-made image to fall flat on its face and eventually to become decapitated. There was nothing left to Dagon but a headless carcass and lots of fear among the Philistines. Harsh plagues followed them everywhere as they continued their plans to hold the Ark hostage. The Philistines were forced to return My Ark to its rightful owners and even accompanied its return with expensive gifts. The Philistines couldn't build gates of captivity that were strong enough to hold Me. And there are no gates of captivity that can hold you either.

Anything that attempts to hold back My plan and purpose for My people will suffer greatly and have no rest until they release it! It was the power of My love for the Israelites that caused the Philistines to relinquish the Ark. And it's still the power of My love for you that will break down every gate that tries to confine you too.

Why not read Psalm 24?

Psalm 24- "Open up ye ancient gates and be lifted up you ancient doors, that the King of Glory may come in. Who is this King of Glory? The Lord Strong and Mighty."

Stop and meditate on the words I said on the Cross: "It is finished!" Selah.

As I hung on the cross and gave My life, the gates of every captivity in your life were broken down. I was the only One who could shatter them. And I did.

My Cross and Resurrection has shattered all forms of captivity, for it was there that I broke the iron gates of death and hell for anyone who accepts Me as Lord and Savior.

I am the King of Glory! And I surely am Strong and Mighty as David proclaimed! I sit on the throne of heaven after accomplishing it all. Every gate of captivity has been broken. Every shackle has been removed and you are free to live for the purpose I've ordained for you before the foundations of the world were set.

What are the ancient gates in your life? What has held you in captivity for so many years? Is it a sin that you hate but still return to time and time again? Is it the grip that someone has over you because you simply can't let go of an offense and refuse to forgive? Does guilt have you constantly within its clutches? Is it the loss of a loved one that's kept you grieving for way too long? Do you feel ashamed? These are all the strong iron gates that David is talking about.

My precious one, it's time now for you to issue a command and say, "Open up you ancient gates!" to all that holds you down. I died so you would have the power to back up your command. Everything must give way at the sound of your voice. I've given you dominion and I, your King of Glory, will go forth with you in victory!

I know your troubles seem as if they have been ongoing for years. Don't let your thoughts defeat you. Those age old problems with fall apart right before your very eyes as you trust me with them. Nothing else needs to be done. They don't stand a chance against My power and love for you. They have to let you go. Their hold over your life has been dealt with. Destroyed.

I devastated every life-confining gate in your life just because I love you. There's nothing that can withstand the power of our command.. I've conquered death itself. What could possibly hold you back now?

Walk with clean hands and a pure heart. Walk clean inside and out covered in My cleansing blood. I'll show you how. Don't lift up your soul to that idol any longer. It hasn't done anything for you but held you down, hindered your relationships, and caused you grief. You've been tied up for too long. I've silenced all the voices that spin in your head and have had the power to confine you to darkness. I've stripped them of their power and I've prohibited them from calling your name. Why? Because you know My Name! The King of Glory!

There's one more barrier in your life that has been demolished. The barrier between you and Me.

Listen and hear the temple veil rip. Selah. Really listen to the dividing wall crumble. You can come to Me with everything. Enter freely! There's nothing you've done that can keep you away.

I am aware, I am compassionate, I want you to come.

You are called for a purpose. You're needed, wanted and valued by Me and the world needs what I've placed within you. Come and let me show you all that's been confined within those gates of captivity.

All the great and mighty things I've planned for you have been hidden behind those walls of limitation long enough. Let Me reveal your real purpose. I Am the author of it. I placed it within you.

You were looking for My purpose when you entered those confining gates. You see, you mistakenly looked in the wrong direction. The lie that relief will come in the form of anger, alcohol, binging, fear, isolation or prescription drugs and even depression is exposed now. You've managed to lock yourself away thinking you finally found something that could block the pain. It's caused you to lie and even hurt the ones you love. You've locked yourself in a place that's built on lies and cheap substitutes for freedom. You may feel trapped and defensive against it all, but today I'm opening you up to solution and truth. You don't have to live there anymore.

The voice that calls you into repeated captivity is gagged by My love for you now.

My precious child, you are free to live the life I created for you. You will finally have joy because all those gates of captivity will fling open, and the gatekeeper will tremble at the sight of you.

Come. Sit. Listen and I will tell you how we can get you to a place of freedom and truth!

Here's what happened: The devil laid a trap for you and you walked right into it. It seemed like the right thing at the time... not so bad... harmless enough. Fun. Right? Until it hemmed you in. Now it has you within its grip. You still long for it and feel comfortable in it. Until it rears its ugly head again.

It's a love/hate relationship. You know you shouldn't, but you do anyway and then shame and guilt comes in like a flood. Empty promises, a sick feeling inside. Yes, you've done it again.

It's a vicious cycle. So much time is wasted on all those thoughts spinning around in your head; the lies and futile attempts to just get some relief. For years you've reached for it and then down you go into a tailspin. You should have known better. How many times can this happen? You're doing the same old thing, slowly working your way back again until the next time.

That's the ancient gate David is talking about! It holds you captive.

Do you want to end it today? How about coming out from behind that gate that has locked you in for so long? I'm not promising you that the temptation to explode in anger, run for relief through drugs and alcohol, or resorting to gluttony will end. No, the temptation will try and lure you back, but what I am promising is that you won't have to fall into your destructive pattern any longer.

All of these things that you try to self-medicate yourself with will be recognized for what they are right at the very moment that they call your name. The temptation will be there, but you won't be a slave to it any longer. You'll have the power to resist every time. And when you resist, it will flee.

Suddenly, the force of the pull is devoid of power. What happened? Why will it be different this time? Because we are going to change a few key things that cause you to fail. You won't be helpless anymore!

What will finally make the difference?

When you decide that your well-thought-out plots, plans and desires to do it yourself will not get the job done, that will be My invitation to come and help you. The things that hold you captive can't be planned away. Stop your calculating and surrender. Tell Me that you're tired, haven't got a clue what to do, and finally out of schemes to free yourself. I am the King of Glory and where I am there is liberty.

Know this! There's a difference between repentance and remorse. Up until now, you've just been sorry that you can't do what you want to do without consequences. That's not repentance.

Change your mind. Hate the thing that's holding you captive. Despise the fearful thoughts that spin in your head and practically paralyze you. Hate what your sin does to others. Hate how it's wrecking your body and shaving years off your life. Hate that you always have to be right. Hate the fact that you are disobeying Me!

What's holding you back and causing these things to continually occur is that you really haven't been sorry. You walk through the gates of captivity willingly, slam the door shut and then cry that you're held captive. That's remorse not repentance.

Here's the key, here's what snapped the chains for Paul and Silas. Here's what summoned the angel to escort Peter out of his jail cell. Ready?

They understood how much I loved them!

That's it! That's all they needed to know. Too simple for you? For those of you who like complicated things, you'll just have to settle for the plain and simple solution. An understanding of My love causes you to strengthen your resolve! Realizing how much I love you changes your mind and causes you to be truly repentant.

When you finally realize the cost I paid to love you the way I do, sinning against Me will be repulsive to you. Every time the temptation rises, you will be reminded that I hung on the Cross and gave it all for you I was tortured for you. Humiliated for you. Whipped and beaten for you.

You'll finally be able to turn around and walk away. I'll take your place in the temptation. My love will hold the door of escape for you. You'll march out! The bars of iron will melt and no walls of captivity will every hold you again.

My love. It never fails.

Linger here. Tell Me you're tired of it. Tell Me you hate it. Tell Me you're sorry, not that you're suffering the consequences, but that you've changed your mind and really hate your sin. Drop your captivity at the foot of My Cross. When you do, you will be saying, "Open up you ancient gates!" And they will open!

TWENTY-FIVE

Making Sense of Inner and Outer Conflicts

– Psalm 25 –

David is seeking Me with a true heart in this Psalm. It was written in the latter portion of his life and is truly an example of how the troubles and sorrow of life should be handled. Notice as you read this beautiful Psalm that he's dealing with the ongoing mental anguish from the assaults of his enemies and also how the memories of his sinful past were still occupying his thoughts.

He was a man who was rejected by many and tormented by people who were supposed to love him. And if that weren't bad enough, thoughts of his own sinfulness were spinning around in his head. He was filled with disappointment in both himself and others. It's a terrible time when outer conflicts and inner conflicts are working in you at the same time.

In the midst of it all, he still found within himself a measure of faith to ask Me to show him My ways, to guide him and teach him My truth. He called Me his Savior that day and I honored his prayers and became the Savior over every area of his life. He received My Salvation Package and relief. Healing and forgiveness were his, just because he came.

Once again as in Psalm 24, he cried out to Me to forgive him of past sins. He said, "Do not remember the sins of my youth and my rebellious ways; according to your love remember me"

As you read on, you will see that he praises Me for instructing sinners in My ways. Guilt was still rearing its ugly head in David's thoughts and he knew that I would instruct him on what to do so he could be assured of My total forgiveness.

Do you need a lesson in how to obtain true forgiveness so you can be free from guilt and condemnation too? Perhaps you do. Today can be the day of freedom from guilt if you heed My words to you.

Psalm 25 is a summary of all David's conflicts, pain and dealings with bitter repentance.

Some of it is an ungodly reflection of things that have been forgiven in his life. But despite David's trouble on every side both from within and without, he finds himself at the foot of My throne to receive all the gifts of love that were waiting for him.

His trouble and emotional pain always drove him to seek My face. Learn from My servant David and bring it all to Me.

Psalm 25:4 "Show me your ways, O Lord, teach me your paths, guide me in your truth and teach me, for you are God my Savior and my hope is in you all day long."

David had nowhere else to turn but to Me. Every path before him seemed to be a path towards destruction. Things that he was dealing with presently were plaguing his mind and the anguish of guilt from past sins were eroding his confidence that I loved him enough to help him. Beware of feelings of unworthiness. They can cause you to doubt that I will help you in your time of need. I will always help you.

In all sincerity, David cried out to Me and beckoned Me to show him the way out of his distress and I knew he was truly seeking My guidance. He really wanted to do things My way. There is a difference between seeking My path and wanting Me to guide you and just wanting Me to validate the choices you've already determined for yourself.

There are some who come to Me with a charted course that they want Me to bless. It's all figured out. They just want My nod of approval. Beware! When you come to Me in this way you oftentimes are substituting My very best and personal plan for your life with a plan that's just mediocre. Even though it might be good, it's not My best and you'll miss out on the abundance that I have to offer you.

David says, "My hope is in you all day long" and you can plainly see that he held true to that statement. He sought Me in the beginning of his plights and followed Me throughout the day, checking in and making sure I was in the center of everything he was doing. I loved that! I honored that!

There are great secrets that can be discovered when you finally come to truly seek My guidance. These secrets are personal, special, and have nothing to do with anyone else. Others just won't understand even if you tried to explain it. I will speak to you in a language that only you can comprehend. I have so many deep and personal things to tell you, things that matter greatly to you and will cause change in a great and mighty way. I want to make specific portions of Scripture come alive in your spirit. They've been written just for you. Yes, they've been written with you in mind. All Scripture is documented for the sole purpose to bring you freedom.

Study the Words of David and other areas of Scripture so I can make them a Word in season and yours forever.

When I give you a Word, no one can refute it. It will settle in your heart, take root and peace will come.

Ask Me daily to show you My ways. Ask Me to teach you My paths and to guide you in My truth. It's the secret to receiving the whole package of My salvation!

I long to be the Savior over your entire life on earth. The Savior of your finances, your marriage, your relationships, your ministry, and your health. Let Me into your day as I've never been allowed before. I AM all you need. Breakthrough will come. Your plan and escape from all trouble and sickness has already been decided. It's time you caught the vision and received the fresh anointing that accompanies it.

David goes on to say, "Remember, O Lord, your great mercy and love, for they are from of old. Remember not the sins of my youth and my rebellious ways; according to your love remember me."

Asked and granted!

Once you come to Me in true repentance and sorrow for your sins, I cover it all with My blood. The flood of My love for you pours out at that very moment! I long to wipe out every wrong and rebellious act you've ever committed against Me.

Listen to Me! There's a difference between true repentance and remorse and not knowing the difference causes great disappointment and a feeling that I don't hear you or want to help.

Let Me explain why I couldn't do anything for Esau even though he cried bitter tears and wept like a child before Me. To everyone else it seemed like true sorrow for what he had done, but I knew that he was really lamenting over the loss of his birthright and how that affected him, not that he sinned against me. It was remorse not repentance.

Remorse rises when you've been found out or heading for the earthly consequences of your actions. You're stuck, exposed, in line for discipline and you want a way out. I know the difference. I look at the heart. A repentant heart understands My love. It rises out of the knowledge that I love you so much and risked it all for you. My goodness and love for you leads to true repentance.

Next time, check yourself. Ask Me whether your repentance is real or not. You may not have known the difference and might have thought you came to Me and asked for forgiveness, but it wasn't repentance at all.

If you're suffering with guilt here's why: Guilt comes where true repentance is lacking. When you come in sorrow and with a changed heart to ask for forgiveness you will never forget it. It's a special time for both of us. And there's no chance of guilt ever rearing its ugly head. When you come and just go through the motions, it may look like you've repented, but we both know better than that.

You might be feeling the way Esau felt and that's ok. If it's just another empty heartless request to help you out with no concern for the deeper things that I long for, I'll even show My mercy in that and get you to a place where you can change your mind. It's all about you understanding My love for you.

It all starts with true repentance. Let's get you to that point. I can change a heart of stone into a heart of flesh. Let Me reveal your heart to you. If you're in a state of remorse and lamenting over a situation where you're in trouble, I'll be right there for you. True sorrow moves My heart.

I will honor your prayer when you cry to Me as Esau did, but it's a much slower process. I have a greater purpose in mind. Come to Me with a sorrowful heart so I can rid you not only of your sin, but also of your potential to do it again. You won't want to sin again because you will understand My love.

David was wise enough to know that My love for Him was "from of old." Did you know that the foundation of the earth also has a foundation? It's My love for you! Before My mouth spoke anything into creation, I spoke My love over you. My great Love has formed a foundation that everything else was built upon. This foundation is the basis of My undivided love for you and it's the answer to all your prayers.

Selah.

David asks, "Who then is the man that fears the Lord? He will instruct him in the way chosen for him. He will spend his days in prosperity and his descendants will inherit the land."

Those who fear Me, which is just another way to say they revere Me, are destined to spend their days in prosperity. You can be assured that if you have a reverence and desire for My ways even your descendants will benefit greatly too! Do something wonderful and pave their way with My plans and purposes.

Does David's trouble sound familiar? He cried, "The troubles of my heart have multiplied. Free me from my anguish!"

Let Me tell you that I have the solution, My dear child. I am your solution. Though your troubles may seem to be increasing, I am there in the midst of them. Hold on. I am right by your side. I will not disappoint you and I will surely come and save you from all your anguish and pain. Let Me help. Trust Me with your life. When you don't know what to do. Don't do anything. Just trust Me.

Is there something that you've done in your life that always seems to surface again and again? Are there sins you've committed years ago that still have the potential to weigh heavy on your heart? Could it be that even though you sincerely thought you were sorry and even felt very troubled about it, that it wasn't My goodness and love that prompted you to come to Me?

Knowing how much I love you is the only thing that can prompt true repentance. Do you really, deep within your heart, know how important you are to Me?

Selah.

Take some time now and let Me fill you with a love that will finally silence those thoughts of guilt and condemnation. Let it pour over you now. You are the love of My life. I cherish you. I don't want you to struggle with feelings of guilt any longer.

Think about my undying love for you all the time. It will flush out the heaviness and guilt and even give you the strength to refuse the lure of sin the next time.

Guilt has no place in you. It wasn't invited into your life by either one of us. Take My hand and let Me walk you away from it. I did it all for you, you know. All of the harsh and brutal treatment at the cross, it was all for you. I didn't just say I love you, I proved that I love you. I poured out My blood for you. My all was given to you that day, and with the same measure of love, I am pouring out My forgiveness to you today.

Let Me sing My Love song over you now. If you listen with your heart you will hear it. Stay a while. Be still now and fully come into My love.

TWENTY-SIX

The Spiritual Microscope: Uprooting What Really Troubles You

– Psalm 26 –

At the first glance of Psalm 26, David presents himself in a manner that could be easily mistaken for vainglory and pride, but that wasn't the case at all. His blessed assurance of advancing in holiness shouldn't be confused with pride. His confidence was quite different from the evil spirit of pride.

This Psalm should be considered a continuation and sequel of Psalm 25, where David poured out his heart in search of the key to integrity and uprightness. David took his walk through life very seriously. He had a desire to approach each situation that he faced with total assurance that he was following My ways. This is the mark of a devout believer.

David was driven by one thing, and that was to have his actions reflect his belief in Me. He wanted to be spotless, holy and empowered with integrity. It was a tall order, but just his desire to be a man of uprightness caused holiness to arise within him.

His high calling to godliness came with many tests of faith and was oftentimes accompanied by the temptation to retaliate and destroy those who were inflicting him with great pain and torment. The lives of his enemies were often spared because of David's quest for holiness.

Because his ultimate goal was a holy life, David was infused with all the virtues he needed to accomplish his desire. All well-deserved retaliation towards the enemies of his soul was relinquished to Me where it belonged. He truly was a "man after My own heart." Just as the sacrifice of bulls and rams in the Old Testament filled the atmosphere with the smell of devotion, simple trust is a sweet savoring aroma in My nostrils.

Notice as you read how David refused to rely on himself or any sinful acts to secure the promises I declared to him through the prophet Samuel. He simply didn't need them. He trusted that if I sent My prophet, I would also guard the prophecy that went forth. His reign as king had been promised by Me and he totally relinquished the protection of that promise to Me also.

In keeping with his quest for righteousness, he passionately welcomed the inspection of his heart. He knew that if deep inner sinfulness is revealed, it is also destroyed. My Glory Light searches the heart and also heals the wounds that generate the sin. By weighing his actions and thoughts against My perfection, he opened himself up to divine direction and grace. He wasn't afraid to have any inner ugliness exposed. He was confident that if he asked, I would reveal any roots of bitterness or sinfulness that was cleverly concealed by a religious spirit.

The greatest form of peace belonged to David because of his true desire for clean hands and a pure heart. Of course, no human can claim to be totally spotless outside of coming under the undeserved favor of My crucifixion, but there's a special deeply seated peace that resides in the hearts of all those who really want to know their faults and have them cleansed by My atoning grace.

In the spirit of prophecy, he describes himself as the bearer of a spotless heart. Pride? No. It was written as a glimpse into the future and prophesies the spotless life that I would live and My obedience even unto death.

The man who walks in integrity and combines it with faith in My Salvation is well on his way to the abundant life. And you can take great pleasure in detecting every act of sinfulness within your heart because the result will be a purifying of your very soul. David knew that I was the Supreme Judge and that nothing escapes My watchful eye. He prays in Psalm 26 that he would not be found among the wicked and spared on the great Day of Judgment. It's a prayer that should be on the lips of all mankind.

David concludes Psalm 26 with the confidence that I heard his prayers. He expresses his delight in My blessings and the blessed hope that he will be among the ranks of those that will sing My praises for eternity.

David achieved the high calling to holiness and the same virtues are readily available to you.

Those I call I will also equip.

Psalm 26: 1—"Vindicate Me O Lord, for I have led a blameless life. I have trusted in you without wavering."

Psalm 26:8—"I love the house where you live O Lord, the place where your glory dwells."

David was crying out to Me in a time of crisis. Famine had broken out in the land and the nation was being chastised for the actions of Saul. Although David was now king, the consequence of Saul breaking the treaty with the Gibeonites was upon them. The Gibeonites were protected by a treaty that was gotten through trickery, but nevertheless it still stood (See II Samuel 21:1).

David's cry to vindicate himself was on behalf of his nation.

Are you surprised that David could call out to me with such confidence and declare boldly that he led a blameless life? Does it seem odd to you that what you know about the life of David doesn't line up with who he claims to be in this Psalm? What about his affair with Bathsheba or the intentional placing of her husband, Uriah, in harm's way, which caused his death? Wasn't that enough to exempt him from calling himself blameless?

David had every right to speak those words. Why? Because they were coming from a heart that truly understood My forgiveness and love. He was a man who said to Me, "I love the house where you live...the place where your glory dwells." He loved to spend time with Me. He loved to come with all his faults, hurts and sinfulness, and work things out with in My Presence. My dwelling was a place where love and forgiveness washed over him to cleanse and heal. He was a free man when he left My chamber.

He asked Me to search his own heart because he understood that a pure and holy life was necessary before he could intercede for his nation. He needed to atone himself before he atoned for the sinfulness of others.

He was responsible for his own actions and knew that they had an impact on the lives of every person who would ever live. He invited Me to search the very core of his heart and desired the virtues that would lead him to a pure and devoted life.

I want you to understand a very important truth. The actions of one person always impact the world. Each one plays a significant role in either the betterment or the detriment of the world. Take your sins seriously, even the smallest ones. The power of agreement with sin, no matter how small, can be deadly.

Bad intentions reside in the hearts of all my people and it's the responsibility of every believer to call on Me to search their heart with the Light of My Glory and reveal the personal sinfulness of their souls.

All evil that exists in your world is the direct result of the refusal of others to follow My ways.

And just as the actions of King Saul caused ramifications to fall upon the Israelites, the sinfulness of others past and present are having a negative impact on your life, your family, your church and your world.

One women singlehandedly wiped prayer from the lips of all children while in their schools. Don't underestimate the power of an individual's decision to agree with either good or evil. Agreement has the potential to destroy or cause miracles.

I'm calling you to realize the potency of your little secret sins and inform others that they play an important role in the welfare of the world too. I respond to intercession, but prayers are often diluted by sinfulness within the heart.

Cleanse yourself before you ascend My Holy Hill.

I called David to a high calling of holiness, and I'm calling you today to the same level of integrity. Do as he did in Psalm 26. Start within your own heart before you search the hearts of mankind and criticize the sins of others. Every major evil act that's happened in the world can be found in the embryonic stage among even the most devout believers.

Things that seem to be mere errors in judgment or minor sins are actually undergirding the atrocities of the world. Little sins are the infrastructure of terrible sins that plague the earth. The pride, hatred, and selfishness that caused the death of millions during the Holocaust can be found in a lesser form right in the pews of My churches, as one believer elevates himself over others or speaks words that wound the very fiber of an innocent person's being.

The hatred and abuse of women is just a more potent form of the tormenting of an unpopular girl in school. The spirit of hatred for women inhabits the playground and every word of gossip spoken at the school bus stop.

The spirit of selfishness that children harbor when they refuse to share, if not corrected or disciplined, is linked to the same evil that allows others to starve to death in many third world countries. A child's sense of entitlement grows to fuel poverty and greed.

Husbands fight against their wives and inflame the evil spirit of hatred to the point where nations fight against nations. Don't you realize that wars within the home are fueling the spirit of war throughout the world? Those who are calling out to Me to intervene in the horrific affairs of their world are entertaining the same spirit in a lesser form right in their homes and local churches.

The secret sin of pornography that satisfies a person for a moment is really giving birth and credence to a world that's filled with sexual immorality. To say "yes" to the temptation and lure of ungodly sexual pleasure is to empower the evil of sex trafficking, prostitution and the exploitation of young children in other nations.

When you read what I say, when I warn you to let your "yes" be "yes" and your "no" be "no" in My Word, let it speak to you about how your little "yes" to a seemingly harmless sinful act gives greater acts permission to exist. Think twice before you withhold justice by just looking the other way. It's the very thing that purged nations from public prayer and worship. Can you sin a little and not have it affect your nation? No, you can't!

I asked the question, "How can Beelzebub cast out the spirit of Beelzebub?" You cannot pray against the very sin that you are committing yourself.

I've told you in My Word that everyone falls short of My Glory. So, understand that each and every one is contributing to these atrocities. Search your heart and make holiness your ultimate goal. Strive for clean hands and a pure heart. You matter and contribute more than you know to either the good or the evil of the world today.

The man that thinks he can come home from a hard day's work and relax as he drinks his way into a blissful state of peace is contributing to the deaths by intoxication and overdoses that are claiming the lives of so many as he sits in his easy chair. "How can it be?" you ask. Agreement with sin is agreement with the death it causes.

I know this is a hard Word, but the call of the intercessor is being silenced by agreement to sin. I've warned you that you have the power to cause the heavens to become as brass and your prayers cannot penetrate the barrier. Your intercession has become impotent.

There are no innocent sins. Each and every one of them, as insignificant as they appear to be, have the potential to undergird and fortify horrific events that plague the earth.

Drop by drop, inch by inch, little sin by little sin, it's all adding up to the overwhelming proportions that you are contending with your world today.

I'm calling you to hate the personal sin that's in your life and pray that others recognize the power that their sinful habits have upon the world.

David asked the question in My Word, "Who can ascend to the hill of the Lord?" and the answer was and still is, "He who has clean hands and a pure heart." How can you obtain hands and a heart that are clean and pure before Me? Run into the atoning pool of My Blood that still lovingly flows from Calvary. Spend time with Me and let me dilute your sins to nothing.

I tell you that after you come to Me in humility and truly seek change from your sinful ways, together we will wipe out the very existence and power of it over your life. My life was given so you could come into a life of integrity and become powerful in the realm of intercession.

Pray your own version of the prayer that you find in Psalm 26. It will let Me know that you desire integrity and purity. Let Me know that holiness means something to you.

Everything has been worked out. Come and find freedom for yourself as well as mankind. Unleash your prayers with a new and fresh infilling of power. Change your world by changing yourself. Begin within your own heart and I'll make you a sharp instrument in My hand that will surgically remove evil from your midst.

Then and only then will you speak and have the authority that you desire. Learn to love My dwelling place. All the great apostles and healers did. Enjoy the searching of your heart. It's where you and I will change your personal world and agree together for the cleansing of the nations. You are welcome and you are called. Come and see yourself so the things you desire to do for Me will work.

No matter who you are, there's sinfulness within the heart that needs to be uncovered and dealt with. Let Me use the tender and vulnerable state that you're in right now to better you and your world. I know your desire for a deeper cleansing is fresh in your heart right now. You want to know and I long to tell you how to purify yourself and feel clean.

Together we can make this time a wonderful experience, an intimate experience and the door to authority in the spiritual realm that you can't imagine. The sight of the blind was restored, the lame walked, the filth of the leper cleansed and it all came from the purity within My heart. As the apostles waited for the power of My Holy Spirit in the Upper Room, they spent their time examining their own hearts concerning all that had happened during My Passion. That is why My power was imparted.

They were serious about purity of heart and so was I. The results were Power and Dominion! Give Me your heart today, so I can gently reveal a sin you never knew existed there.

Don't be afraid. I will love it out of you. I've waited for the day that you said yes to the deep and inner cleansing that I desire for you. Today could very well be that day! Selah.

TWENTY-SEVEN

Getting Off the Emotional Rollercoaster

– Psalm 27 –

Psalm 27 speaks of intense faith, desire and expectation. As it unfolds, it reveals the roller coaster of emotions that were waiting for David at every turn. But his emotions and all the circumstances of his life were also filled with a personal and solemn promise and a true devotion to Me that were tested every day of his life.

The day of his secret anointing by My prophet Samuel was a marked event that would uphold him through the worst of his challenges and fears. The trials he faced would have killed an ordinary man devoid of faith, but his anointing for kingship was a promise, a vision for his future and the target of his focus through the worst of times. Who could argue with My promise that he would someday occupy the throne and that I would be with him all the days of his life?

My Glory visited him the day of his anointing and his ability to wait in confident expectation was his greatest weapon against every individual battle. Saul's vicious death threats and relentless pursuit of David's life couldn't usurp My promise and neither could the death of his child, the heavy pangs of guilt, or the rejection of Absalom.

David was a man of clear vision. He knew where he was heading, that I was right beside him all the way, and that not one of My promises would go unfulfilled. Through all the ups and downs and emotional upheavals, David was confident of one thing. He was surely on the side of victory! He knew he wasn't going to be swept away by the fierce waves. My promises would not be mocked under any circumstance. There was no valley too low for My strong arm to rescue him and he was never elevated to a position where he forgot who brought him there.

Though his countenance vacillated from faith to fear, and rejection was like a sword piercing his heart, he always returned to the blessed assurance that he would recover from every harsh blow of the enemy. David knew I was his Guiding Light and his Salvation. He knew My dwelling Place was a shelter for him and that I would raise him up above his enemies every time he found himself in trouble.

David opens this writing with a proclamation of sheer confidence in My ability to secure victory and it has become the same source of strength for many believers today. As you read, you will be taken on a ride of emotional highs and lows only to once again come to the conclusion that David knew so well. Confident waiting on Me is the key to peace and the abundant life.

Compare David to the desperate and lost prodigal son of the New Testament and how they longed to return and dwell in the house of their Father. As they found themselves at the point of no return, there I was to welcome them into their heritage once again. The account of David's and the prodigal son's lives were documented so you would have hope and rely on Psalms like Psalm 27 to lift you up and into a place of peace no matter what your circumstances may bring.

Allow Psalm 27 to penetrate your heart deeply today. Allow the message that's strewn with shifts in David's countenance to speak to you. As he goes from confidence to despair, and from doubt to faith, realize that I am there whether you are elated with joy on your mountain top of victory or devastated in the valley. Expect the tide of emotions to carry you right into My arms.

Psalm 27:1-"The Lord is My Light and My Salvation, whom shall I fear? The Lord is the stronghold of My life of whom shall I be afraid?"

What were the first Words I uttered in the book of Genesis? Wasn't it "Let there be Light!"?

Before the foundations of the world were set, the earth was a desperate place, and in its present state displayed none of the purpose and potential I planned at all. It was filled with darkness and needed one thing above all to penetrate its hopeless condition: My Presence. It was desolate and like all forms of darkness whether physical, emotional or spiritual, the earth was desperate for Me to come and intervene; to bring order to the chaos.

The entrance of the Words "Let there be Light" brought forth life. The earth was infused with My presence and from that moment, it was bursting with potential. The Words I spoke and the Light of My powerful Glory joined forces to rid the world of chaos and futility.

Genesis isn't the only place where I revealed Myself as the Light. Think about the Light and brightness of the fire and My Glory cloud that lead the children of Israel as they wandered in the wilderness. My Light and Glory came together as their solution too.

What about the radiance of Moses' face after he spent time with Me on the mountain? He was saturated in the

Light of My Glory when the cloud settled over Mt Sinai. I long to do the same for you, My precious one. I long to lead you out of your wilderness and call you to My mountain where I can speak to you as I did My friend Moses. The Light of My Glory is available and plentiful. I am the Light of the World!

It was the same Light of My Glory that David was longing for in his times of need. His cry generated from a heart that was truly desperate in this Psalm. Not only was he trying to escape physical death, he was also desperate to escape the paralyzing fear that set its sights on his thought life. Spiritual war was set against David, and the constant change of emotions at every turn was taking its toll on him. He would have gone absolutely mad unless he called on Me to intervene. His world was filled with darkness and void of everything except self- preservation.

He was struggling to merely survive.

I know you feel the same way at times. You feel as if you're just going through life in a mode of survival and glad to make it through another day. Are you satisfied with just existing and skimming by? That's not the life I planned for you. I long to be the Glory Light of your world, too, and to bring abundance and peace into your life. I long to fill you to overflowing so you can concentrate on giving and loving others instead of merely stamping out fires in your own life. A life of self-preservation is a terrible way to live.

You have gifts and talents and a vital role to play in My grand strategy for the world. I need you to break loose from all the areas of your life where you haven't found peace. All those areas where pain and sorrow have made their home need My Glory Light. Let's get the things that occupy your mind settled down. Once My Glory Light flows, you'll never be the same. It will gently fall over your past where unnecessary guilt and shame live. The warmth of My love and forgiveness is all the relief you need to move on.

My Glory heals your wounds. Those tender areas of your soul that have been injured so badly will be no more. I'll cover your ears to the repeated sounds of hurtful words that have been spoken. I'll blind you to the things you've seen that you shouldn't have. I'll draw a curtain over the things that have happened and cover your thoughts so you can live and move and have your being in Me. Peace and restoration is here.

I want you to receive My Glory Light just as the desperate world did at the beginning of time. It was such a pivotal point for the world when My Light entered on the first day. There was hope!

My Light and Presence came and My desire unfolded into the earth. It will be pivotal time for you too when My Glory flows right to the very point of your need. You too will be filled with hope!

David was sure of My Love and the powerful Light of My glory, and you should be too. He called Me his "Light and his Salvation" in Psalm 27. My Light and My Salvation are inseparable, you know. I'm the Savior and Victor over everything that comes your way. He asked "Whom shall I fear... Of whom shall I be afraid?" What are you afraid of? Stop and think for a moment. That's My point of entry into your heart.

Do you want Me to cripple that fear in your life instead of allowing it to have its way with you?

You have imprisoned yourself with it. Just receive My Glory Light and be healed now. Receive My glory. Open up and receive. I am right here to pour it over and within you. I want you to become just as radiant as Moses. Won't you let Me shine My Glory and bring warmth into all those cold areas of your heart? If you let Me in, all the age-old strongholds that were erected within you will give way and collapse under the power of My love for you.

When I walked the streets of Jerusalem, the Light of My presence fell upon the hearts and souls of so many. It was My Presence and My Words just as it was at the beginning of time. As I traveled through the countryside, sin, sickness and torment couldn't withstand the Light I brought to those I met along the way. Lives were changed. All afflictions and shame were brought under My power and miracles were released from heaven. It was the powerful Light of My countenance and the Words of My lips that destroyed everything that caused pain.

My Glory Light has not diminished. It will overwhelm every form of darkness and void in your life. I want it to and it will be so. Hold on to that.

So what do you want Me do for you? Where should My glory Light go?

Why don't you just let Me enter into your heart where all sorrow tries to hide? I'll travel through you, just as I traveled through Israel and all your wounds will receive a touch of My Glory. Even the ones you don't know exist.

It's a wonderful day for you. A new fresh anointing is replacing all that has been washed away. Now you have the same Glory Light within you that filled the earth when it brought forth creation. You've been made new. The agent of change you need has come. Rest now.

Everything's going to be all right.

TWENTY-EIGHT

Tell Me What You Want

– Psalm 28 –

Civil war had come upon David's country. It was a time of national crisis. David's Psalm, although it is short in length, is long on his quest for righteousness.

At the first glance, it appears that King David is spewing out all forms of hatred against his enemies and is even mistakenly referred to as an "imprecatory" or one that calls down curses or wrath against evil doers. But these words don't come from a man whose passion is revenge. David's character was far from one who took retaliation into his own hands. Even his enemy Saul, who was a relentless pursuer of David, knew his life was spared because David refused to lay a hand on him. Saul was well aware of the nature of David and you should be too, so you can view the Psalm from the perspective on which it was written.

David was a man who hated evil, both within himself as well as in others. He was a prayer warrior and My prophet. He knew the power of his words! He spoke, prayed and prophesied that My righteous ones would be spared from the tactics of the wicked and also that My just judgment would eventually come upon all workers of iniquity.

Psalm 28 is also a prayer for himself. As he looked deep within his own heart and his past, he knew that he too was not exempt from falling into the snares of the enemy. He cried out for Me to save him from the infectious lure of sin that can so easily entangle even the righteous.

As you read this short but very potent Psalm, go deep within it and not only acquire the heart of a true believer who loves Me, but also one who hates evil with the same level of intensity.

It's not enough that you love Me, you must hate and take a stand against the evil of your present age. Eli, the Priest, was complacent and did nothing while his rebellious sons took for themselves the meat from the pots that were offered up as a sacrifice to Me. Turning your eyes away from evil is condoning it and as serious as committing the crime yourself.

Evil will be purged from your midst if you take a stand against it and defend My ways before all mankind.

Don't keep silent. Silence is destroying your world.

I sit at the right hand of our Father waiting for His command to go and bring His children home. As I wait, I am in constant prayers of intercession on your behalf and will continue to make My request that the righteous are kept from the wiles of the wicked and protected until I come for them. And I will continue until you are with Us in Paradise!

Psalm 28:1- "To you I call O Lord, my Rock ...For if you remain silent, I will be like those who have gone down to the pit."

David's beloved country and kingdom was being ravaged by war! And His beloved son was the instigator of it all. Absalom had convinced the crowds that He should be hailed king and without hesitation all but a few of David's loyal subjects joined forces to dethrone him. They rejected

David and all he stood for. He was dismissed, rejected and despised. He found himself homeless, on the run and overcome by his broken heart.

David's life was thrown into a frenzy and when his world was collapsing all around him, it wasn't long before he cried out to Me in desperation. He needed strength, he needed stability and he needed shelter so he called Me his "Rock." He said, "To you oh Lord I call." He called and I answered! I heard his life-forming words and became his "Rock" as soon as the words left his lips.

The very thought of My turning a deaf ear or remaining silent to the cry of David was like being thrown into the pit of hell. He cleaved to his prayer time because that was where we spoke to one another and he received relief from all that troubled him. I want you to know that I could never turn away from the cry of My beloved. It's not in My nature to ever ignore your cry. Use your mouth and call out to Me! Now, might even be a good time for you to talk to Me about what's going on inside you. I'm here to listen.

Understand this. There's power in what you say! I've given you the gift of crafting and creating your world with the words you speak. Every word you release accomplishes something. It's up to you whether it's for good or evil.

I hear everything you say and so does hell. When you speak life, I move. When you speak words of death and negativity the enemy is empowered. So much agony and defeat is fashioned by a heart that lacks understanding of the truth I'm revealing today. When you speak, the spiritual world responds. That's why I've warned you that you will give an account of every idol word that's spoken and encourage you always that you can move mountains with the very words you pronounce.

My prophet asked that a hot coal be placed at his lips to prevent him from speaking words that had the power to backfire upon the earth. You can set a situation on fire with what you say and literally destroy a person with a word. And your words don't stop from accomplishing things after they disappear from you hearing. They continue to accomplish what you set them forth to do, just like My Words.

What you seem to think is innocent talk is not the case at all. Your words are like hammers and knives and are often the weapon of choice to devastate My people. Watch what you say! You possess a lethal weapon! Innocent people can become your targets and are being maimed and wounded by the assaults that leave your lips. It's not innocent. It's a matter of wounding a heart that will relive it many times over.

I've filled your heart with My love. Why not release it over those who are around you and cause healing instead of deep painful wounds. You certainly are equipped to do it. Your words can carry My healing Balm of Gilead to others. Encouragement that can propel a wounded soul forward is within you. Someone might not take their own life because of what you say. Your thoughtful words and songs are the vehicle by which My Spirit travels into the hearts of the hurting.

Now that you have a better indication of the power that's within you, can you see why you are called to speak life? Damage is done to the agenda of the enemy of your soul every time words pour from your mouth in prayer, thanksgiving and praise. It's really your heart speaking and, when you praise Me with the fruit of your lips and I will pay attention.

If you don't think I hear you or that I am remaining silent as David did, ask Me for a vision, confirmation, and peace within you. Let Me give you a blessed assurance that will appease all your doubts and fears.

I have told you that My precious loved ones perish because of their lack of knowledge of who I am and how much I love them. I don't want you be in darkness any more concerning My attentiveness to your every need.

If I need you to wait, I'll give you a Word that will see you through. You are not in this alone. I'm here and if you ask, I will lift the curtain and show you an inward picture of what will surely come about. There's no need to be left in the dark. Let Me reveal a promise that's found in My word that will see you though. I have written and blessed you with Scripture promises so you can stand strong and "speak life" while you wait for the absolute perfect time for Me to release your blessing and victory.

It's hard to wait, but not when you have My Word within your spirit, it will fight every doubt and challenge every conflicting thought. If you doubt that I will do it, get your Bible and come to Me. Praise will be the fruit of reading My Word. As you're taking in the promises that have been secured by My death, praise will arise in your heart. You cannot come to Me and ever walk away without being filled with praise.

When fear was gripping David so intensely that he doubted I would ever bring the victory, he knew what to do. He lifted his hands towards My Most Holy Place and began to praise Me. His praise became warfare and a powerful weapon against his enemy.

Think of Moses on the mountain while Joshua fought in the valley. Every time Moses lifted his hands towards Me the battle was won. Every time David lifted his hands in praise he too came closer to the restoration of his kingdom. It's the same with you. Every time you lift your hands toward heaven, something will shift in the spiritual realm and cause the wall that blocks your victory to crumble.

Call Me by My Names! I have many and each one is a testimony of who I long to become in your life. Your Light, Deliverer, Repairer of the Breech, Strong Tower, Defender, Lover of your Soul. All these Names are Mine for you to behold.

Learn about them and use them to light a fire under your prayers.

Learn from David in Psalm 28. Even when thoughts of being forgotten and alone plague him, he called on Me through the power of praise. He couldn't remain in the grip of feelings of abandonment. His thoughts of My silence were quickly rectified. As he praised Me, truth took its rightful position, and he was once again assured of My love for him and the truth that I would never think of being silent and not answer him.

Remember, that the only One that was ever brought to a place of being forsaken was Me when I hung on the cross. I was abandoned so you would never be.

"When you call, I will answer and show you My Salvation!" I've worked it all out! My plan to see you through was costly, but you are worth it. I sacrificed My life because I love you. It was all done for you. So you need not fear or ever feel alone.

Because of My sacrifice on the cross, I've made it possible to hear every one of your cries for help. I've pulled down every dividing wall between us. You have access to My throne room. The gates of heaven are open and I hear you.

Because you believe in Me, I will rescue you each and every time, and I will never stop showering My love, protection and grace upon you. You have hope because you call on Me. Speak to Me with your words of power! Let's create healing and deliverance together with our words for you and your loved ones.

What I did for David, I will do for you. Tell Me what you need today. I'm waiting to hear the words of your heart.

What do you want Me to do for you?

You have My undivided attention.

Tell Me what you want?

Selah.

TWENTY-NINE

Let's Change Some Things

– Psalm 29 –

Psalm 29 is a call to adoration and praise! It was written to expand the understanding of the believer and exemplifies how even the most powerful forces of nature are no match for My grandeur and authority over all the earth.

Once again, David satisfies the "surface" reader of the Psalms with peace as well as the believer who searches for the deeper meaning within his writing. He displays his own personal contentions with an actual violent storm that threatened his life, but also embeds within this Psalm a confidence in My ultimate final victory over all evil and wickedness. If you look closely, you will find a vivid description of how My final return will impact every creature of the universe.

David's expressions of peace were the aftermath of his previous Psalm where he thought he would perish with the ungodly in a national disaster. Psalm 29 is the conclusion where David found himself, once again, within the powerful grip of My protection and grace.

As the tempest winds blew and caused the earth to shudder and convulse, David's heart was composed and he could only give Me praise because he knew that even though the earth would give way, he was safe within My powerful grip of victory.

Whether I'm found to be the Contender of the storms of your personal life or the final raging Storm in the last days, you can find comfort within Psalm 29.

David knew that when the storms of life begin to surface and surround every aspect of his life with a violence that seems to have no match, that My love Storm would surely appear on his behalf. At the perfect time I came and wiped out every contention in his life. The effects of every evil storm that tried to dominate his peace had to give way to My Tempest of Glory.

In order for My Word to remain true, there must be an abhorrence of evil. There is no perfect love without the total hatred and intolerance of wickedness. It's My nature to Love passionately and it's My nature to despise evil.

David speaks of My final Storm of justice that will rip through the earth and shake down everything evil in its path. It will devour the mightiest of worldly powers that support evil and cause everything wicked to brace itself against its intensity, but to no avail. I'm going to take you way above it all, where great peace and stillness are found.

As you read this Psalm, look with a heart that is confident in David's prophecy of My upcoming judgment. When I return, I will expose and annihilate every form of wickedness and rebellion and all the things that caused you pain and sorrow. It will all be devastated and My followers will rise above My execution of judgment to a place of peace and joy.

They will celebrate My verdict when I wipe evil from the face of the earth and bring them to a life that's wonderful and everlasting.

It's coming, and the reality of My triumphant return should bring you to a level of peace that causes you to become unshakeable in all situations. Grasp a new level of confidence from Psalm 29. Allow it to give you the peace and confidence that will move you to a new level of faith and trust. Receive a new understanding of My majesty and with it will come an undeniable peace that will carry you through until My return.

Psalm 29:3-4-"The voice of the Lord is over the waters; the God of Glory thunders, the Lord thunders over the mighty waters. "The voice of the Lord is powerful. The voice of the Lord is Majestic."

Psalm 29:10-11 "The Lord sits enthroned over the flood, the King is enthroned forever. The Lord gives strength to His people, the Lord blesses His people with peace!"

My voice is powerful! My voice is majestic! My voice is everywhere!

Before the beginning of time, chaos responded to My voice and obeyed My command to flee from its inhabitance. I spoke, and all necessary elements assembled in order to form your great and vast universe.

My voice has been heard by many of My faithful believers. It revealed truth to My prophets and informed Abraham and Sarah of the personal event of the birth of their son Isaac. I dispatched angels to proclaim the birth of John the Baptist and filled My mother's heart with the news that I was approaching the earth, that I would take on flesh and blood and become the anticipated Redeemer of the world.

As I walked the earth, the sound of My voice healed people, evicted demons from dwelling within them, and raised the dead. My voice was the spark that initiated miracles. It commanded the raging storm to "Be still" for the apostles, and it resounds over every troubled water in your life. At the sound of My voice, angels stand at attention. They exist to respond to My voice.

David was still running for his life at the time of this writing and his troubles ran as deep as the ocean. Not only had his trials mounted, but he also found himself physically caught up in the torrents of a mighty and treacherous storm.

He was bracing himself within a violent tornado and also being thrashed from one emotion to another as everything in his life was being tossed to and fro with a violent rush.

Physically and emotionally David needed Me to save him or he was doomed. As the lightning flashed and his breath was taken away by the waves of fear that had the power to pull him under, he heard My voice. He heard it echo over the waters of his despair. My powerful voice reminded him of the truth that no matter how traitorous the physical or emotional storm may be, I sit high and above it all. My Power and love for you overrides anything you're going through. All that I am is at your disposal. All the chaos and turmoil is beneath Me. There are no threats of impending danger.

My Presence holds back evil and creates a blessing wall around you that cannot be scaled. Let the storms and floods rage, they have no power over Me or you! Everything that lashes out at you will be struck down and paralyzed by My voice. I "sit enthroned over the flood" and I live to have My voice speak on your behalf. Floods always represent rebellion in My Word and I surely am enthroned above every evil uprising. That means that everything that tries to rebel against My perfect plan for your life will suffer at the hands of My justice.

My voice silences all other voices. They wouldn't dare continue their assaults in My presence. "When you call, I will answer and show you great and mighty things." The evil against you can only shrink back and become impotent before Me.

Do you remember when they came for Me in the Garden of Gethsemane armed with their best soldiers who were arrayed with swords, clubs and all sorts of weapons? I asked them who they were looking for and they responded "Jesus of Nazareth." I said three words" "I Am He!" and they all fell back onto the ground and were rendered helpless before Me. No man could ever overpower Me. The crucifixion was My choice!

Peter thought he could defend Me by merely cutting off the ear of a soldier, but My voice was empowered with the authority of legions of angels. A single one of them could destroy nations.

There is nothing I need from mankind. I am self-contained and all-powerful. When you realize this truth, you will fear nothing. There won't be anything, no matter how intense to move you from your position of peace.

When David declared that My voice was over the mighty waters, once again his message had multiple implications. He was not only professing My authority over every individual circumstance, but also over the wickedness of all mankind.

Search My Word and you will find that floods and raging waters were always stilled as a believer called upon My Name. Every form of rebellion will be dealt with either by repentance or destruction. I caused Noah and his family to survive the deathtrap of the consuming flood, and I will also save My believers from the destruction that will surely come in the End.

I will exert My prevailing Words for you if you want Me to. Let Me shut the mouths of the evil hungry lions who seek to devour your peace, finances, health and loved ones.

Daniel's devouring lions surrendered and so will yours. Let Me silence and disgrace everything that refutes My will for your life. When I speak everything will fall on its face and declare that I am God.

When David declared that I sit above the mighty waters. he was showing you the place within your heart where you too can sit above all that tries to claim your life. There are no storms in My presence. You heart can be stilled and will be stilled as you listen to My voice that's found in My Word. As you read My Word, you will become fortified and confident that nothing can hurt you anymore.

Where I live there is peace and My abode is within you. I reside in the temple of your heart and sit on the throne that you have erected for Me with your praises! I am truly within you and long to arise out of your belly and burst through with a flood that brings life to everything it touches.

I've chosen to have My powerful voice heard through you. You are My mouthpiece! Everything you say has power. The thing that sets you apart from all of creation is that your voice contains authority and influence. When you speak, My power backs up every word you say.

Didn't My apostles command the lame to walk and the sick to receive healing? My voice was within their voices. I promised them that if they declared it, it would come to pass. Take hold of your promise and speak! Did you forget that I have promised, if you "say" to any mountain of a situation, to be removed that it will uproot itself and be thrown into the sea of nonexistence? I want My voice, the voice that every demon must acknowledge, to be within your voice. This isn't a concept. It's reality.

Speak. Don't be afraid. Let Me and all that hell is raging against you hear your voice! What they will hear is My voice.

Open your mouth! They will have no recourse. They will have to submit to what we say together. Speak life to your situations and death to everything that is against it.

You can do this! Be assured that I will arise and resurrect My plans for you if you obey Me and speak. Violent storms will subside and My purpose will take root. I promise.

Let's change things together for the better. Choose a portion of My Word and speak it out loud and often. It will save your life!

What powerful force in your life needs to be dispelled by My powerful glory? Stop and think and tell Me in your own words.

Does your new understanding of My power through Psalm 29 give you the assurance that I am a matchless force that will arise and cause evil to depart?

Talk to Me about it while the truth about My power and glory are fresh in your spirit. Selah.

Is it a new concept for you to know that you are worth fighting for? You are!

Do you realize that I will move hell itself to free you from any chains of rebellion that block your abundant life and peace?

All the things you desire to escape from whether they have been done to you or by you, will be overcome by My Glory. Come and sit with Me and it will depart. Let Me fill you until all you want to escape from flows out and never returns. Selah.

I won't stop until you can praise Me as David did. Your victory will be as Triumphant as his. I promise.

THIRTY

Dance

– Psalm 30 –

Finally, the sentiments of David's heart were an accumulation of peaceful emotions and perfected faith.

In Psalm 30, David found himself reminiscing about all that transpired in his life. It was a life filled with one tumultuous adventure after another, and heartbreak and desperate cries for help were common to him. But the conclusion of it all was the gift of a relationship that was now rooted in deep trust and steadfast faith. His heart was filled with thankfulness for each and every day of his life. Even though times were extremely difficult, his soul was at peace because the results were greater than he could have ever imagined.

The theme of David's life was one reoccurring battle after another. The circumstances would often change, but the Solution was the same. Many life-threatening situations led him to utter despair, but he always came to the conclusion that Someone more powerful would see him through.

As he scans his life in Psalm 30 and reflects on the great and terrible things that occurred, he once again offers up praises to the One who saved him from it all. His heart was filled with gratitude for the relationship that was forged through those times with the Creator and Keeper of the Universe.

Finally, all that was left was a call to worship and adoration for My faithfulness to him and his descendants. He now stood on the other side of some drastic events and with each testimony of My goodness, a path was paved for greater trust in Me than ever before.

All of his enemies were overthrown. He remembered Goliath crashing to the ground in defeat and the freedom from Saul and Absalom's assaults. He shouted praise for the events that led to the restoration of his kingdom.

He remembered the freedom that came when he wept in remorse over his affair and the restoration of his heart after the death of his precious child. He was brought out of the pit of despair with a heart filled with thankfulness.

He remembered the building of his own house after his life as a fugitive was finally over. It was a special house because it represented freedom from his enemies and the conclusion of his life as a fugitive.

He remembered the day the Ark of the Covenant returned from the house of Obed-Edom and how he danced in celebration at My faithfulness. Even though his son Solomon would be the overseer of the construction of the Temple that would be a permanent home to the Ark, it gave him great joy to contemplate its completion.

He remembered the many days that were filled with adoration and praise that followed the dark nights when he didn't think he would live to see another day.

Psalm 30 is a conglomeration of all the wonderful events that transpired during David's long life and how the sweet reality of My forgiveness, peace and victory filled his heart.

Psalm 30 is the song of David's heart to thank Me for turning around all his dark and desperate nights and bringing total Joy in the morning. It's a manifesto of praise that calls you to a new level of hope and encouragement too. Your dark nights will also blossom into days that are filled to the brim with utter joy. This I promise you.

Because of the special times we've spent together over these 30 days, you now have a better understanding of how My heart longs for you. You've learned of My undying love and how I long to lift you up and out of any storm that comes your way. All the trials and tribulations that have made you cry and tossed you to and fro have all led you to hear My call and draw closer to Me through the pages of these love letters. Now you can see that what I've done for David, I will surely do the same for you.

Let's read what David says to both of us in Psalm 30. I want you to be mindful of how he lifts up his praises to Me and then adds some very worthwhile advice for you.

Psalm 30 is a wonderful blend of glorious adoration and heartfelt advice. It was written for you and Me, and we can both celebrate it together.

David sings, "I will exalt you, O Lord, for you lifted Me out of the depths and did not let My enemy gloat over me. O Lord My God, I called to you for help and you healed me. O Lord, you brought me up from the grave; you spared me from going down to the pit."

My dear precious one, this is what I long to do for you too. To lift you up out of the depths of what you're going through. Take hold of My strong arm and let Me lift you out of your depths of despair. I want to touch the most painful thing in your life right now. Let Me lift it out of the broken area of your heart. Just relax and feel it lifting now.

As it lifts, I want you to feel the healing and comfort that I'm applying to the areas you've given Me during our times together. As I anoint you with My healing Balm, I want you to feel a new measure of life filling your heart. That's where the damage was done and that's where I have My nail scarred hand right now. I purchased this healing balm with My love blood. It's the answer! You don't have to suffer any more.

Now allow it to slowly penetrate and go deep within you. Sit and receive it now as the healing anointing flows into areas that need a touch from Me. Take a minute, relax and receive.

David said, "Weeping may remain for a night, but rejoicing comes in the morning." When I felt secure, I said, "I will never be shaken."

I want you to realize that I've been with you through all your pain. I know it doesn't always feel that way, but all the while I was singing songs of love over you. And I'll never stop. You wouldn't have made it if I didn't keep you within My watchful eye. I cried when you cried. My heart broke with yours. I really was there when that hurt settled deep within your heart. I began your healing then and want to conclude it today.

There's nothing that can't be healed.

I've waited for you to come to Me in this special way and now, here you are.

David said, "You turned my wailing into dancing, you removed my sackcloth and clothed me with joy, that my heart may sing to you and not be silent. O Lord my God, I will give you thanks forever."

When broken hearts are repaired, they sing for joy because they know that something new is on the horizon. I have something in My hand that I've held for the entire time that we've been together during these special 30 days. I am opening it now and releasing My Glorious Light of Love. Feel its warmth and healing. It's radiating ever so lovingly on those dirty rags that you've been wearing. I'm removing them as you stand in the glow of My love for you. I'm taking them off you and dipping them in My love blood. Watch as they become radiant before your eyes. They're garments of joy now. Let Me adorn you with your new garments.

They're made especially for you. I'm pleased. You're cherished. And your garments are radiant with things that only you and I know about, right? You are the love of My life. Look at you! You're beautiful!

ACKNOWLEDGMENTS

Lord, I Am Grateful.

*L*ord, I am so grateful to You for surrounding me with a community that has been personally chosen by You to be a part of the development of this devotional. You have graciously sent so many wonderful and gifted people as instruments of encouragement and assistance to me and for this, I will thank You always.

I thank You first and foremost from the deepest part of me for my husband **Fiore**, whom You know has been a continual source of support for me throughout my life and who, just like Jesus, exemplifies a life of selflessness and unconditional love. He has proven over and over again that a life that emulates Yours is possible through love, support and simple kindnesses.

Thank You, Lord, for the tremendous impact **Frank** and **Joan Dursi** have had on my life and for my children and their spouses: **Robert, Lauren, Andrew, Michael and Leah**. I love them and their children **James, Daniel, Matthew, Anthony, Drew, Noah, Jacob, Kristen and Paul, Riley, Elijah and Brooklyn** so much and I am forever grateful You have blessed me with them.

I thank You, Lord, for the prayer team You have assembled. Thank You for **Miss Genevieve Connell, Sister Faye Richardson, Winnie Ihemaguba, Toni Ann Russo** and my dear sister, **Peggie Byrnes**, whose petitions of prayer have been invaluable to this project. The effects of their diligent intercession will surely be felt in the lives of our readers for years to come.

Thank You, Lord, for sending much needed assistance and an excitement for this project through **Karen Miglin** and **Catherine Kelly**.

All of these precious servants who love You so, have truly made the path of Your will for this book both easier to find and peacefully endured.

I thank You so much Lord for blessing me with the help of the very special **Chris Dillon**, and also for gifted author **W.C. Bauers**. (www.wcbauers.com) They welcomed me into and helped me navigate the complex and uncharted waters of the literary world. Their support, professional advice and just being there for me is truly appreciated.

I thank You, Lord, for **Christopher Cervelloni** of **Blue Square Editing** and also for the wisdom and insight of **Mark Malatesta** from thebestsellingauthor.com.

Lord, You have blessed me so much with the special kindness and support offered by **Monica Schmelter**. She truly is a beautiful person both inside and out and her sincere and genuine kindheartedness and enthusiasm will be cherished always. Thank You for her, Lord, and bless her.

Thank You, Lord, for the firm foundation of Your truths instilled in me by **Pastor Carol Galagos**. Her insight, keen discernment and wisdom has been a tremendous inspiration to me and has impacted my life and ministry beyond words.

*Lord, You have surely blessed this devotional with a caliber of creativity from the heart of **Mary-Ann Ellsworth** that overwhelms me. Thank You so much for her and **Truth Boost LLC**. Mary-Ann's love for You and her dedication to serve You are unsurpassed and I will always be grateful to You for blessing this project with someone as beautiful and gifted as she. (www.truthboost.com)*

*Thank You, Lord, for **Lisa DeSpain** and **Margo Bush** from **Bush Publishing**. They have surely made the mechanics of book publishing a joy and I appreciate them immensely!*

*Lord, I cannot begin to thank You for my beloved **Christian Faith Fellowship Church** which is pastored by **Reverends Tom and Diane Feola**. They have, because of their love for You, continually provided a platform for me and scores of others to serve You and your people. Their dedication and heart for the lost have caused true and lasting life change in the lives of so many. Thank You for their service and impact on our community and beyond. Thank You for allowing me to be a part of it all. (www.cffchurch.org)*

But when all is said and done, I praise You Lord for giving all those mentioned their very life and breath and blessings and grace to assist with this devotional. You gave them life so they could breathe life into this book. I could never thank this community enough so I am asking You to rain down blessings upon them for me. To You be all the glory, honor and praise forever and may You be glorified in each and every reader's life. Amen.

About the Author

Jeannie Settembre serves God's people both within the church and on the streets of the inner city. She hits the streets in impoverished areas to bring hope to the homeless and many others living in desperate and dangerous situations. She is also a credentialed minister assisting Christian Faith Fellowship Church in the areas of empowering women through the Word of God, community outreach and teaches and speaks at women's retreats and conferences. Writing daily devotionals is a natural progression of Jeannie's passion to see the desperate become filled with hope. Jeannie is married to her husband Fiore, has three grown children and enjoys a large family with many grandchildren. Jesus changed her life and she longs for others to experience the love and nurturing only the Lord can give.

To reach Jeannie Settebre, visit her website at:
www.30VisitsWithGod.com

Join Jeannie Settembre in her NEW online course:

The Mission Outside Your Front Door

Course includes instruction in:

- Developing Community Outreach Through Partnerships
- Surveying Community Needs
- Producing Local Outreach Events
- Urban Outreach
- Identifying Your Passion to Serve Others
- Mobilizing Servant/Leaders Around You

**For more information,
visit Harrison Bible Institute online at:
www.HarrisonBibleInstitute.com/**

Harrison Bible Institute

provides online education in 8 courses of study:

- Biblical Study Program
- The School of Business Education
- Pastoral Study Program
- The School of Global Missions
- Christian Ministry Program
- Youth Ministry Program
- Children's Ministry Program
- The School of Music

CHRISTIAN FAITH FELLOWSHIP CHURCH

PRAYING . GOING . LIFE-CHANGING

DOWNLOAD OUR APP
SEARCH CFFC

LIKE US ON FACEBOOK
SEARCH CFFCNJ

FOLLOW US ON TWITTER
SEARCH PASTORTOMFEOLA

WATCH US ON YOUTUBE
SEARCH CFFCHURCHVIDS

3188 ROUTE 94, FRANKLIN, NJ 07416
973.209.7786 | WWW.CFFCHURCH.ORG

bush
PUBLISHING
& associates

www.BushPublishing.com